Tired of TEEN ANXIETY

A Young Person's Guide to Discovering Your Best Life (and Becoming Your Best Self)

BY
LISA COYNE
SARAH CASSIDY

Tired of Teen Anxiety

A Young Person's Guide to Discovering Your Best Life (and Becoming Your Best Self)

Published by:

Pavilion Publishing and Media Ltd
Blue Sky Offices, 25 Cecil Pashley Way
Shoreham by Sea, West Sussex, BN43 5FF

Tel: 01273 434 943
Email: info@pavpub.com
Web: www.pavpub.com

Published 2024

A catalogue record for this book is available from the British Library.

ISBN: 978-1-80388-275-8

Pavilion Publishing and Media is a leading publisher of books, training materials and digital content in mental health, social care and allied fields. Pavilion and its imprints offer must-have knowledge and innovative learning solutions underpinned by sound research and professional values.

Authors: Lisa Coyne and Sarah Cassidy

Cover design: Emma Dawe, Pavilion Publishing and Media Ltd

Page layout and typesetting: Emma Dawe, Pavilion Publishing and Media Ltd

Printing: Independent Publishers Group (IPG)

Praise For This Book

"**TIRED OF TEEN ANXIETY** *is without doubt one of the best and most helpful books on anxiety in adolescence I have ever read! It's absolutely packed with brilliant, powerful and simple exercises that have the potential to radically transform the way adolescents understand their experience and relate to their anxiety. Beautiful and articulate – a brilliant and heartfelt contribution to the literature!*"

Duncan Gillard, author of *ACT for Dummies*

"*Engage your curiosity, become skilled in living your best life and be your best self – we would all benefit from that! For young people living in these anxious times,* **TIRED OF TEEN ANXIETY** *shows them step-by-step how to create their life. If you know a young person who is anxious, or you work in any professional capacity with young people, this book is a fantastic asset. Get it on your shelf, share it in class, and give it to your own kids.*"

Louise Hayes, PhD, author of *The Thriving Adolescent*

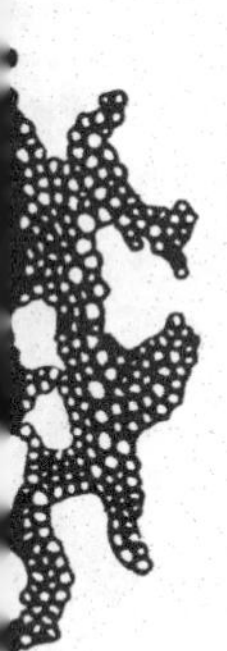

*"**TIRED OF TEEN ANXIETY** has that wonderful quality of a book that talks to teenagers without talking down to them. Rather than hitting teens over the head with their message, the authors encourage their readers to be curious and open while making the argument that anxiety is something to live with, not fight against, in order to become your best self. A must-read for any anxious teen – and their parents."*

Regine Galanti, PhD, author of *Parenting Anxious Kids*

*"**TIRED OF TEEN ANXIETY** is a remarkable self-help guide tailored specifically for teenagers struggling with anxiety. It combines the wisdom of ACT with engaging exercises, making it an excellent companion on the journey to a happier and more fulfilling life. The language is clear, relatable, and jargon-free. Teenagers and their caregivers will find this book to be a compassionate and essential guide."*

Professor Louise McHugh, University College Dublin

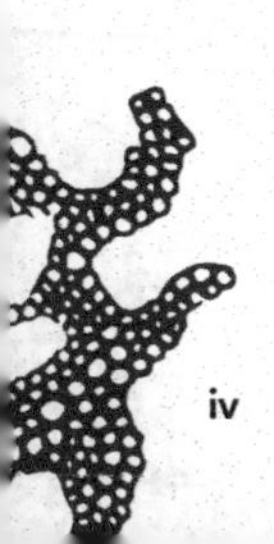

Contents

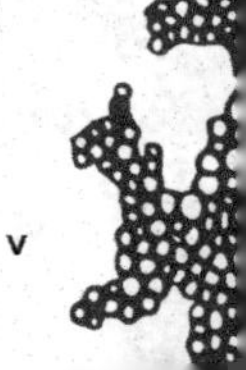

Special Dedication

We'd like to dedicate this book to our very dear friend and colleague, Dr Meria Dolan, CAMHS Clinical Psychologist, County Meath, Ireland. Meria cared very deeply about first and foremost her family, child and adolescent mental health, the arts and also the integration of artwork into mental health spaces. While she is tragically no longer with us, she has touched so many lives with her extraordinary kindness, gentleness and humour. She will never be forgotten.

Special Thanks to Our Art Club Teens on Both Sides of the Atlantic

This book would not have been possible without the generosity, talent and patience of our Art Club in Ireland (you all know who you are so we don't need to say your names) and the students in Melrose High School Art classes: Hannah Jones, Leah Mallozzi, Rosalie Martin, Lena Micciche and Elm Moock. Thank you for your extraordinary artwork, and for reading and giving opinions on all the versions of this book. We'd also like to thank Natalie Bricker for her keen copy editing, Susan Jerz, and Sean Shinnock for guiding our young artists in graphic design. To our young people who helped: we are constantly inspired by you as you make your journeys, and we hope you keep it up. From the bottom of our hearts, we thank you for sharing your stories with us and with each other, and we sincerely hope you like the final book. It wouldn't be half as good without all of your expert advice along the way. This book is for you.

Not forgetting...

Many kind thanks to Louth Meath Education and Training Board, Athboy, Co Meath, Ireland, and especially to Serena Duffy, for endless generosity and flexibility in making the building available so Art Club projects can take place. Small communities really can do big things when we put our hearts and minds together. Thank you also to Sarah Cunningham and JJ Luz Macabacyao for showing up every week and bravely exploring art and anxiety with us, and to Dr Roberta Hines for always being willing to coach us in the background.

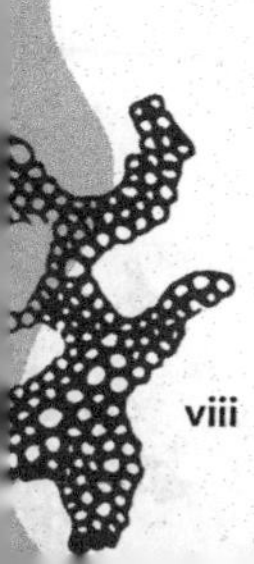

Hello from Us

HI, I'M DR. LISA and I not only help kids with their anxiety, but I've also worked through my own! I live near Boston in the United States with my family (Josie and Rory, this book is for you), three dogs, Doog, Lemon and Peach, and a horse named Mac. My wish for you is that this book helps you know you are not alone, and helps you find your strengths – because they have been there all along.

HI, I'M DR. SARAH and I live in Ireland with my three kids (Patrick, Alfie and Elizabeth), two dogs, one rabbit, two ducks, one bearded dragon and one bearded husband (Kevin). This book is for all of you. I wrote this book because I have been anxious all my life and it has taken me most of my life to figure out how to live my life anyway. I'm so glad you're holding this book right now and I hope you keep reading it.

Foreword

Hi, I'm Natalie! I have anxiety – and if you're reading this book, you probably do, too. Perhaps you've even read a book about anxiety before. I've read many, books about anxiety, and the one thing they all have in common is: they don't eliminate anxiety. It's still with you. But that doesn't mean it has to be unbearable. In fact, I bet that after you read this book, you'll find that the heavy load of your anxiety has lightened a little bit. At the very least, you'll walk away with some new coping skills and a clearer understanding of what's going on in your brain.

This book won't cure your anxiety, but it will prompt you to think about it in new ways that can help you gain perspective. It will lead you through some really helpful tools, and I promise it's not a boring textbook. It's been written with you in mind – not parents, not younger kids – you! I encourage you to give it a try, even if you have any doubts about reading something that's supposed to help with your anxiety. The worst that could happen is you carry on like normal. But the best that could happen is you learn something helpful.

Welcome to *Tired of Teen Anxiety*. I've learned a lot from this book, and I have a good feeling that you will, too.

Natalie Bricker
College student experienced with anxiety coping skills

Introduction – Let's talk

Hey there.

We suppose somebody – probably a parent, therapist or other caring adult – picked up this book for you and put it in your hands. Or maybe you went searching for it yourself. If you're reading it, we're guessing that anxiety is pushing you around. Maybe you're feeling overwhelmed, or isolated, or like you need some help – or maybe you don't feel like you want any help. Maybe you don't want to talk or think about it at all. Maybe you're sick of feeling the way you have been, and resentful that you're standing or sitting here with this book in your hands.

For what it's worth, we're glad you're holding it, and we really hope it's useful to you. We didn't write it to waste your time. We also didn't write it to 'fix' you, or anything about you. And we *definitely* didn't write it to give you a load of rules to apply to your life, or to tell you what to do.

We're guessing that you're struggling with anxiety, and that it sucks. We're also guessing that you've been feeling it for a long time, and that maybe you try to hide it or keep it to yourself. Maybe you've had it since you were a kid. Maybe it's new. Either way, it's probably not something you're super excited telling all your friends about. Maybe you don't talk about it at all.

We don't know. We can't read your mind. But what we can do is…

- Tell you that if any of this describes you, then you're not alone. One in three people, over the course of their lives, will struggle with anxiety. So, the next time you're in class or out at the shop, count. Every third person you see will have, or already does have, the same struggle you do.
- As we speak, about one in five of the young people around you also struggles with anxiety. The rate of anxiety in teens *doubled* after the COVID pandemic. The number of therapists who treat anxiety *did not*.
- If you're struggling with anxiety, you probably feel pretty down and depressed. That's because there's a strong relationship between anxiety and depression in young people (three out of four teens with depression also struggle with anxiety).
- Very few teens with anxiety get the help they need.

Help can be hard to find. Sometimes it's hard to let on that you may need help, and harder still to ask for it. Sometimes there isn't money to pay for help. Sometimes you might not know that what you're experiencing isn't just what happens to everyone in life. But that's one of the reasons we wrote this book.

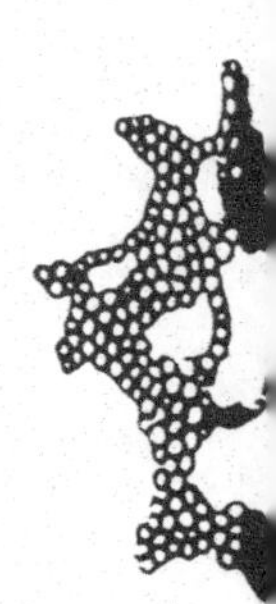

We want this book to help you. In it, you'll find good, solid, evidence-based information about what anxiety is and isn't, why avoidance gets us stuck, and how to grow flexible, curious and strong so that you can find your way into a life you love waking up to every day. We'll give you the goods, and you can choose how, when, and if to use them. That part is up to you. So consider this an opportunity to try something different and to let in some guidance, gently offered, and see where it takes you. We think and we hope that you'll try it all out.

What we can tell you is that those teens who do try out the tools in this book – with their whole heart – start living their way into a life that feels good, real, and free. Often, they start to enjoy being in their own skin. It's not easy, and it's not magic. And no one gets it exactly right. But the principles and skills in this book are based on scientific evidence. What that means is that they've been tested as part of treatment research studies involving hundreds of kids, teens and adults, and the majority of people who use them consistently, especially in therapy and afterwards, come out better in the end.

One thing to understand is that this book, just by itself, may or may not be enough to help you get a lot better. There isn't yet data on that. What it can do, however, is help you to understand and practice strategies that work with anxiety and OCD. For some of you, using this book may be a first step towards seeing a therapist with regular sessions. For others, it may be transformative by itself. You can take this stuff, run with it, and you're good to go. Whatever the case, we hope it sets you on a journey to your liberation and into a life that you're excited to wake up into every day.

There's one really important idea we want to introduce: having anxiety does *not* mean there's anything wrong with you. Anxiety is just part of being human. If you're struggling with it, that means it's time to get curious about how you can 'drop the rope' in that tug of war. So when you feel like anxiety stops you in your tracks, we think it's time to explore other ways to handle how anxiety is demanding all your attention.

First things first. What do you know about anxiety? If you're like most people, you've learned from the Internet, or TikTok, or maybe from your friends, if they talk about anxiety. Perhaps you've learned something through popular culture – like films, music or books. Maybe you have a parent who also seems anxious to you, which might be the case since there's a fifty percent chance that one of your parents struggles with anxiety too if you're an anxious kind of person. Most of the messages you've seen are probably that anxiety is bad, that it needs to be managed, that it's harmful and that it's a sign of weakness. And you generally receive these messages in a very loud way, especially when you can't get rid of them.

Unfortunately, most of those messages are way, waaaay off. But they *feel* true, and it's what everyone else says, and maybe it's what you think too. Well, luckily for you, we don't care about that. We do care

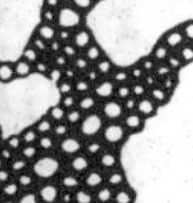

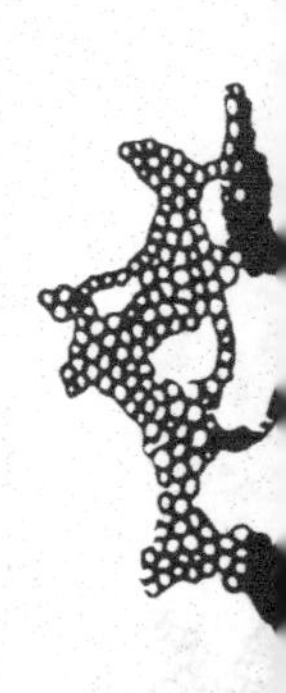

about what behavioral science tells us about anxiety, and what the purpose of anxiety is, and do you know what else? That in truth, anxiety in and of itself isn't the problem here. Trying not to be anxious – or avoiding anxiety – *that's* the problem.

Now, you might be thinking – this sounds crazy!

You're right. It does sound crazy. The idea that anxiety isn't a problem – or at least, that it doesn't have to be one – sounds counterintuitive. But you're going to have to dig a little deeper into this book so we can lay it all out for you. And we'll try to do that as quickly, and as clearly, as we can. We'll also suggest practical skills that you can put into practice as soon as you read about them. This book is very much about learning as you go. It isn't about believing us just because we wrote a book; it's about trying out the things we suggest and seeing how they work for you, in your life.

This book is all about developing a different relationship with your anxiety. It's about learning to face your fears, especially when not doing so makes it impossible to live your best life. But it's not just about doing the stuff that worries or scares you. It's about *how* you do that stuff – with openness, and self-kindness, and willingness to let yourself feel and think whatever shows up inside. As you might imagine, this can feel really challenging, really hard. And it's probably the last thing you'd ever want to do, especially since it's likely that you picked up this book to see if it offered ways of getting rid of anxiety.

We wish we could help you with that. But the fact of the matter is, we can't. That's right, you heard us right. We can't help you get rid of your anxiety. Nobody can. Take a few moments to reflect on that. How long have you been trying not to be anxious? Weeks? Months? Years? Most teens who have anxiety start experiencing it in childhood. Have you been able to get rid of it? For good? Sure, avoidance – trying not to think about it, pretending you're okay, restricting the places you'll go, maybe even doing some kind of ritual to 'undo' or 'fix' anxiety – might seem like it works. But does it? Is your anxiety gone for good? We're guessing no. After all, you're reading this book. Right? Uh-huh. That's what we thought.☺

We're here to show you an alternative to avoidance. We hope you'll think that the tools we offer are worth taking for a spin. After all, what could possibly go wrong? (Don't ask your anxiety! If you do, the answer will probably be, "Everything!"). Here are a few suggestions for how to make your way through this book.

First, be *open*. We know that you know lots of things, and we're guessing that you don't love feeling patronised or talked down to. Still, even though we understand that, here's one place we're going to ask you *not* to be an expert. You see, if you're an expert, there's no room for learning or anything new! It might feel good and a little safer if you feel like you know everything there is to know about anxiety. But at the end of the day, it isn't possible. You're kind of in a sealed room with your anxiety if you think you

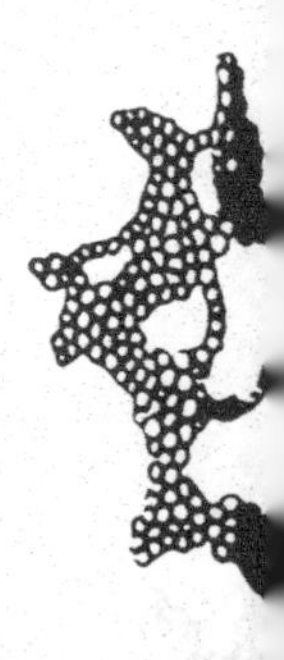

know everything about it, with no way to get out or let anything in. So instead of acting like an expert, see if you can keep a *beginner's mind*. Pretend you're new here.

Be open, even if your mind wants the certainty of knowing it all (minds are like that – more on that soon!). In the mind of a beginner, there are many possibilities.

Second, cultivate *curiosity*. What we know about mental health is that for teens, one of the most important factors in psychological well-being is… drumroll please… curiosity. In research, teens described by their parents as demonstrating curiosity experienced better mental wellness. What does it mean to be curious? Try the things in this book. Ask questions. Look for things that surprise you. Question assumptions you have about your anxiety. Wonder whether there might be something to be learned here. Put down the stuff you've been trying already, especially if it's stuff you've tried over and over again and it hasn't really moved your anxiety needle much.

How about you give the ideas in this book a shot and see where they might take you? See if, maybe – just maybe – they might liberate you.

Third, we want to talk about *secrets*. Anxiety and obsessional worries and fears, they love secrets. And the closer you hold those secrets to your chest, the more power they hold over you. The more and bigger pieces of you that you keep hidden, the less of you is available to be known by your friends and your family.

Again, we're not telling you what to do here. But we hope that you won't let anxiety tell you whether and how you connect with those that are important to you. You're a magnificent human being, worthy of love and connection, worthy of really being seen and known just by virtue of being you. If anxiety has stolen that from you, then it's our deepest wish that you can win it back.

Don't let anxiety silence you. We hope the words in this book will help welcome you back to the world, to your people, your community. You belong here with all of us.

Our final wish for you is that you'll discover your own strengths, the ones you had no idea you already had, and win your freedom from anxiety. We hope that once you've wound your way through our book, your anxiety no longer matters. We hope that you'll be firmly on your way to building a life full of lots of other stuff that matters way, waaaay more.

Best wishes to you, our reader. You've got this.

We believe in you.

Lisa and Sarah

P.S. About your parents...

Although this book is for you, we did think it was important to include some guidance for your parents. We hope that you'll pass along our book to them, with the next page dogeared so they can read it. It may, in the long run, help them be better advocates and supporters of you as you work on building a freer, richer, more you-sized life unconstrained by anxiety.

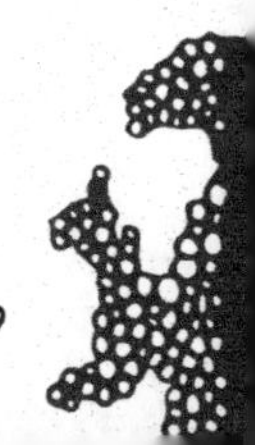

A quick note to parents (or other trusted adults)

Dear Parents,

If you have an adolescent who is struggling with anxiety, it can be really hard to know how best to help them. Moreover, while there are lots of books and other forms of guidance for parents of younger children, resources thin out for the parents of teens. Yet supporting a teen through adolescence is a whole new level of challenging, and requires a shift in the parenting strategies you may have used when your child was younger. You might feel stuck, lost, or at an impasse – just like your teen does.

There are no silver bullets here, and change takes time. Still, here are a few key ideas that may be useful to you.

- Slow down and take a moment to settle. Parenting adolescents struggling with anxiety is *hard*. It's not you. It's genuinely challenging, and it will ask more that you feel you can handle sometimes. It's okay for you to think that, to feel that, to say that out loud. No parent feels like an expert at this.

- There *are* things you can do to 'scaffold' your teen as they learn how to tackle their anxiety. It's important to remember that in adolescence, your child is building life skills – and the best way for them to do that is to try things out, with your support. This involves *letting them feel their anxiety, without rescuing them from it.* We know. You're thinking, *yeah right*. But please don't close the book. We're quite serious, and there's a lot at stake for your child here. Let this idea roll around in your head for a while. Consider it.
- In order for your child to build a sense of self-efficacy, they most need two things from you:
  - *Empathy and validation*

    Their experience is the truth. Know that they're doing the very best they can, with the only tools they know. Understand that stubbornness often reflects desperation, and that to stop doing what they're doing – to lean into their fears instead of avoiding them, for example – feels terrifying and impossible. They aren't doing it for attention, or to be disrespectful or oppositional. They're doing it because it feels like all they've got. We hope to give them some more effective, very powerful tools in this book.
  - *Your confidence in them*

    Often, teens come to us unable to see the strength inside of them. It is so helpful if you, their parent(s), treat them like you do see this. Gently, kindly, express this when you can. You

can say things like, "I can see how worried you are, and I know you'll be able to handle this", or "I hear how hard this is for you, and I know you'll get better and better at facing your fears." Note that empathy without confidence, or vice versa, is less effective than both ingredients together.

- When you're the parent of a teen, you may feel like they won't listen to you, or that what you think doesn't matter to them the way it did when they were small. But please know that you, and your relationship with them, is just as important now as it ever was, even if it doesn't seem so. To keep communication open, it can be more helpful to listen than to speak. And if your teen won't talk with you, simply try to stay in their orbit. It can feel thankless, trying to stay present and open when your teen does all they can to, well, be a teen and give you monosyllabic responses. Keep it up anyway. You do matter. You matter a LOT.
- It's okay for you to ask for help in supporting your teen. Bringing up a child with anxiety requires special skills that may sometimes go against what you think of as good parenting (remember we encouraged you to let your teen feel anxious without rescuing them? Yup.). Mental health counselors with specific training in Acceptance and Commitment Therapy (ACT) and Cognitive Behavioral Therapy (CBT), including Exposure and Response Prevention (ERP), can help. The principles and practices we've included in this book are from these interventions, which

research has shown are effective with anxiety and OCD. There are even programs *just for parents* of anxious children that have demonstrated good outcomes for young people (e.g., SPACE). You don't have to go this alone. For more resources, check out this website: https://anxietyintheclassroom.org/.

- Finally, take a breath. Be gentle with yourself, whatever you're thinking and feeling about all of this. We parents can be very self-critical when we feel we can't solve anxiety for our children, or when we can't protect them from distress. You're walking a path that many parents have been down and are still walking, even though you may feel alone. Take care of yourself. It's hard to support your teen if you yourself are compromised. So we encourage you to check in with yourself throughout the day, and ask yourself *What do I need right now?* Maybe a cup of tea, a few minutes alone, a few pages of a book, or just to sit down and close your eyes. Maybe go outside and feel the gentle rain on your face, let the sunshine warm your back, listen to the wind in the trees. Put on a favorite song. Call a friend or family member. Whatever small practice helps you to feel connected or replenished, please nourish yourself as you walk this path with your teen. We've been there, too. And we are with you.

With kindness,

Lisa and Sarah

1: Getting curious about your anxiety

When you're scared of something, you try to get away from it, right? The last thing you probably do is stop, look around, and get curious about it. But what if getting curious is exactly what you need to do?

Have you ever felt really scared but you didn't know why? Maybe you felt jittery or shaky, or had butterflies in your stomach, or felt stuck, like you absolutely could not do something that you needed to? Have you ever worried a lot about how people might judge you? Or have you ever worried about what your whole existence was even about? Like, what even is your purpose and meaning in the universe? Have you been the kind of teenager who worries about the future and has lots of thoughts that start with "What if?" – and end with catastrophic things your mind imagines up for you? Or are you perhaps a teen who tries hard to be perfect, and worries that if you can't get things *exactly* right, then you must be worthless?

Does any of this stuff sound familiar at all? If it does, then you might have experienced how these kinds of thoughts can spiral. It can be really difficult to know whether or not you'll belong or even what's happening in the world. You might ask questions like: "What if I fail my exams?"; "What if I don't get into college?"; "What if the environment becomes unlivable?"; or "What if I'm not actually a person?"

You might start to panic, or you might even start to feel completely separate from yourself or experience any number of really uncomfortable sensations that can go along with anxiety.

Well, it turns out that lots of teenagers have this thing called 'anxiety', and it comes in lots of different shapes and sizes. Of course, if you're experiencing it, it probably feels enormous to you. But the interesting thing about anxiety is that, while it often feels really uncomfortable, there are some situations for which we actually need it.

Let us tell you what we mean by that. You see, anxiety has a purpose: it actually mobilizes the body for threat. This means that, if there's something dangerous in our environment, anxiety helps us react very quickly to these threats. So our anxious responses are often trying to keep us safe.

However, what do most people tend to do with their anxiety? Do they recognise that it's a threat detector trying to keep them safe? Not really. Most of us

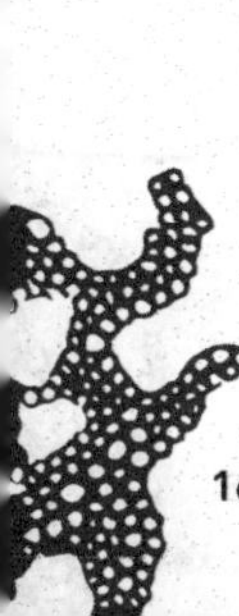

notice that our threat detector is switched on and then we use it to avoid *every single thing that might possibly be a risk*. When anxiety shows up, we try to avoid taking risks altogether – by telling ourselves not to do things, for example, or by trying to keep things the exact same way. We might also overthink everything, or we might be very impulsive and do things without thinking at all.

You see, when we start to avoid the things our anxiety alerts us to because it thinks it's keeping us safe, it's kind of like anxiety builds a cage for us. So instead of making anxiety go away, it's trapping us inside it! Or you might even think of it as a YouTube or TikTok show called 'The Anxiety Channel', which you're watching all day long. What's your anxiety doing now? How are you going to screw this up? And then your life becomes all about watching life go by outside the cage. Anxiety becomes your zookeeper.

Or perhaps your anxiety is like a partner. They say that the person you're in a relationship with is the one you spend the most time with. So maybe for you, that's your anxiety! And maybe you're super tired of listening to it, and you try to avoid it at all costs. But here's the thing: by trying to avoid it, your attention is actually on it ALL THE TIME. The more you try to get it to be quiet, the more it talks to you. Does this feel familiar?

Exercise 1: My anxiety and me

So, what we'd like you to do now is to think about these metaphors for your relationship with your anxiety and see which one feels like it fits best for you.

Come up with a metaphor that feels like it fits your relationship with your anxiety and, in the space below, describe that relationship. Is your anxiety a zookeeper? Is it an annoying partner, an unwelcome party guest, or an irritating backseat driver who comes on every trip with you and won't keep quiet? Come up with anything that works for you. You can write, doodle or draw – that part is up to you. You can even make up a short story or a song!

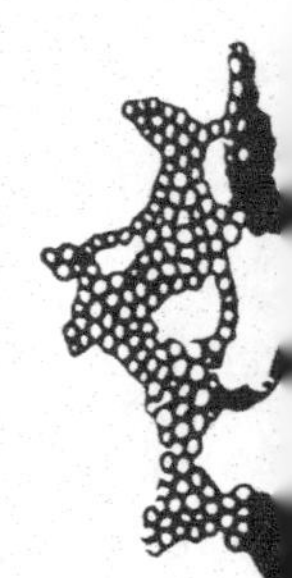

Next, we'd like to know *how* what you do to avoid your anxiety works. Does it actually keep you safe? Does trying to avoid feeling anxious work? We'd be willing to bet that it doesn't. I mean, if it did, you probably wouldn't be reading this book, right? See if you can slow down and get curious about your anxiety.

Exercise 2: Does avoidance work for me?

Can you tell us about some times when you tried to manage, get rid of, control, lessen or avoid your anxiety, and what happened? Not what you think *should* have happened, but what *actually* happened when you tried to make it go away? Write or draw about it below.

For most people, trying to control their anxiety is like standing on a beach trying to hold back the tide with a bicycle pump or a toothpick. These things just aren't really possible, are they?

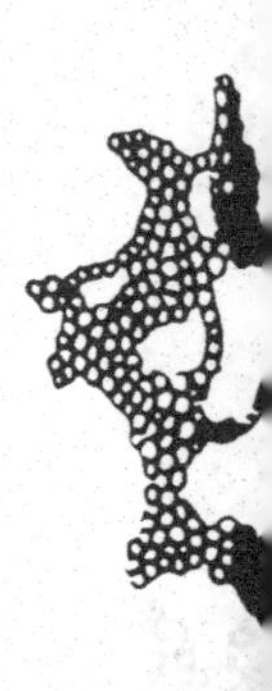

Slowing down and stepping back

Let's take this idea a bit further. What are the side effects of trying to limit or control your anxiety? Have you noticed that when you try to control it, you have no ability to focus on anything else? Strangely, when you're trying to control your anxiety, it often makes it feel bigger. In fact, it feeds it. You know what else? When you try to avoid anxiety, it also keeps you from learning anything new about it.

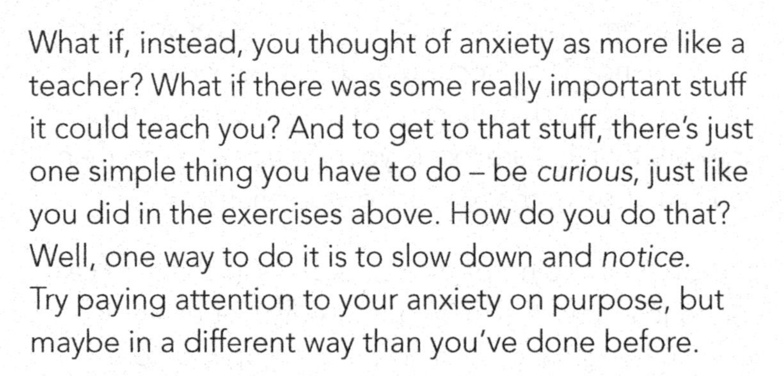

What if, instead, you thought of anxiety as more like a teacher? What if there was some really important stuff it could teach you? And to get to that stuff, there's just one simple thing you have to do – be *curious*, just like you did in the exercises above. How do you do that? Well, one way to do it is to slow down and *notice*. Try paying attention to your anxiety on purpose, but maybe in a different way than you've done before.

Before now, you've probably been trying to control your anxiety, or perhaps it's been trying to control you to keep you safe. But instead, what if we listened, carefully?

Think about all the things you do with the ocean when you're at the beach. You watch it – maybe, like us, you watch it for hours. You walk the shoreline looking for shells. Maybe you watch the light change as the sun rises or sets. You listen to the sound of wind and waves, of the breakers drawing back and rolling little pebbles. You feel the sand in your hands and under your feet, and you sift it through your fingers.

You smell the tang in the air, the seaweed along the tideline. You taste the salt on your lips, like tears.

Another way to be curious is to step back and notice what you are thinking and the emotions you are experiencing, which is a bit different than just, well, thinking and feeling.

What does it mean to 'step back'? Well, have you ever daydreamed, and gotten lost in your thoughts? And then maybe a teacher or friend tapped you on your shoulder and you came back from wherever you were in your mind? That 'coming back' is what we mean here by 'stepping back'. You can daydream, completely unaware that you are lost in your thoughts… and then you can observe that you are daydreaming.

Turns out, stepping back is a helpful skill that you can use to learn more about your anxiety. For example, you might notice your mind bringing up memories of being at the beach in the past – maybe when you were small, or walking your dog, or surfing. You might observe emotions arising inside you as these images and memories come back – maybe savoring them,

maybe allowing yourself to wade in, just a bit. You might also notice that the ocean looks different all the time, depending on the wind, the light, the weather, and maybe even the different phases of the moon.

We don't normally do this with our anxiety. We don't slow down, step back, and pay attention to the details of it. We've been taught not to. We've been taught that anxiety is bad, and that too much of it means we're weak. So we try not to think about it, not to acknowledge it.

But what if you'd been taught that the ocean was bad, just like anxiety? Yikes! Imagine how your experience of it might change. You might avoid going to the beach altogether, and instead stay home imagining how horrible it is. How empty would your story of the ocean be if you couldn't properly look at it the way we did just there? Wow. What a loss! You'd be missing so much of the magic. And here's the thing. It's true that the ocean is sometimes scary. And anxiety can feel that way, too. But as we've discussed, the more you avoid something, the scarier it gets, especially in the absence of letting yourself learn about it. So, let's get curious again.

Let's try exploring our anxiety the way we just imagined we might explore our experience of the ocean while at the beach. Take your time and try on for size as much or as little as you like. This is probably new for you, so be patient with yourself as you explore and experiment with us.

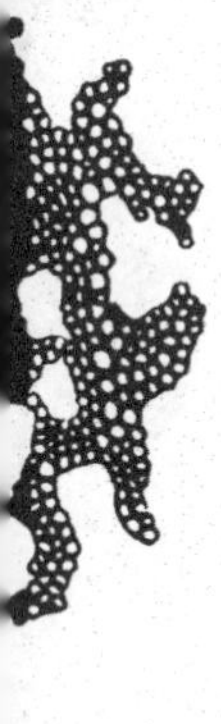

Exercise 3: Where my anxiety lives

Let's practice this idea of stepping back and noticing anxiety and the feelings that come with it. In the outline of the body that follows, indicate where your anxiety lives. Where are its edges? Make a note of whether or not you could feel it as we spoke about it earlier in this chapter. Did it have a color, or a shape perhaps? Did you have any urge to control or avoid it?

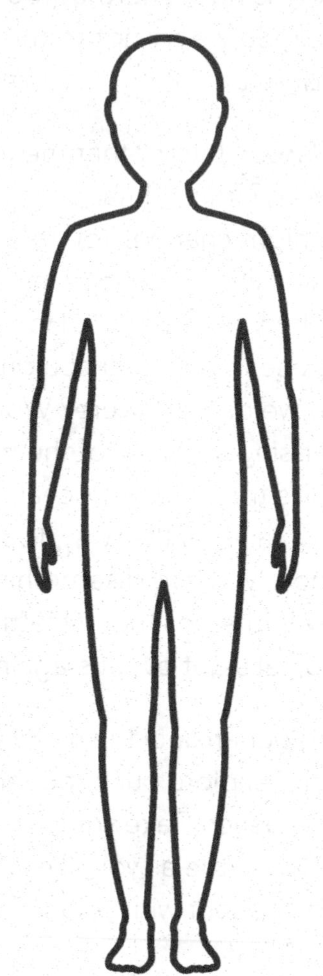

Thoughts, feelings and sensations

Hey! We're glad you're still here!

What have you noticed so far? Are you having any big thoughts coming up when we keep asking you about your anxiety? What does your mind say about your anxiety and the things we've been saying about it? What about your body? Does it have any big physical sensations, or feelings, or emotions?

It can be hard to put these things into words, but it is important to try. So see if you can slow down, step back, and tell us a bit about what you usually experience in the following circumstances.

When I get anxious, I have the following thoughts:
(No editing allowed – tell us everything your mind tells you!)

When I get anxious, I have the following emotions and physical sensations:

(*Still no editing – tell us everything you feel!*)

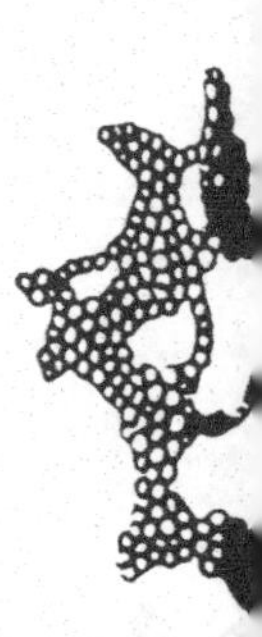

Exercise 4: How do the different parts of my anxiety work together?

Now it's time to put everything we've learned so far together. Below are three circles – one for thoughts, one for emotions and one for physical sensations. First, we'd like you to write the thoughts, emotions and physical sensations you described above into the circles. Then, we'd like you to draw arrows back and forth between them when you notice that one might lead to another, because we suspect you might notice as you do this activity that that often when you have an anxious thought, it leads to an anxious sensation – or when you have an anxious sensation, it leads to an anxious thought. Label this flow between the circles.

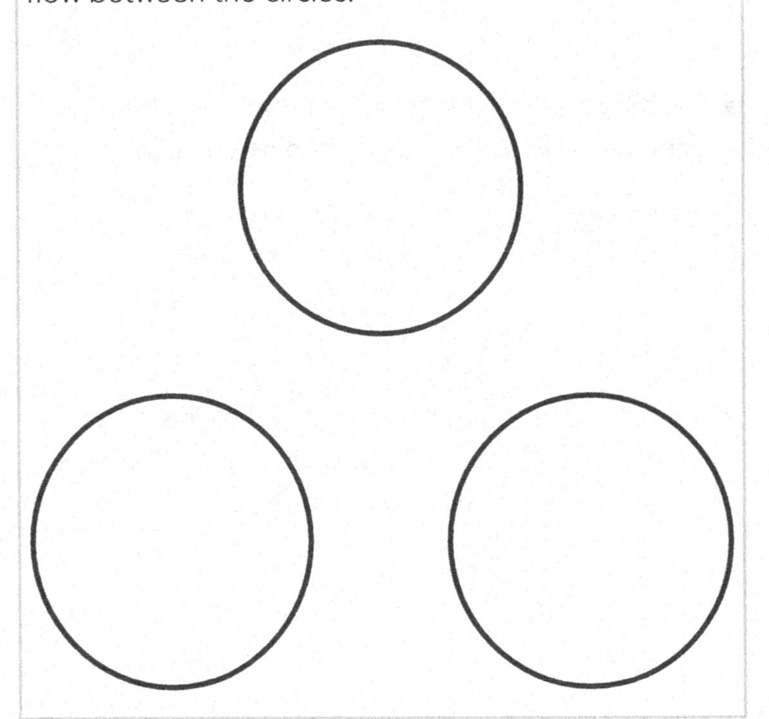

Okay, let's do some writing. Now that you've got curious about your anxiety, let's take it up a notch and get creative. What if you imagined your anxiety like another person?

Exercise 5: Characterizing my anxiety

Let's describe your anxiety like a character in a novel. Really try to imagine this by answering each of the following questions:

- What characteristics would your anxiety have? Is it repetitive? Is it afraid of taking risks?

- What does it think about your ability to handle things in the world? Does it think you can do it?

- What's your relationship to it? Who's the boss? I mean, really? Is it you or your anxiety? Tell the truth, come on! You can trust us. ☺

- When your anxiety tells you what to do, do you do it? Based on that, what assumptions do you think it makes about you? About your strengths and weaknesses? About what you can and can't do?

- If you could hear your anxiety talking, what would its voice sound like?

- If it had physical characteristics and a style, what would it look like? How old is it?

- If you've known it for a long time, what might it do if it came into your house? Like, would it look in all your cupboards? Go straight to the fridge? Eat all your food? Crash on your sofa? Open TikTok and show you terrifying stories of impending doom? →

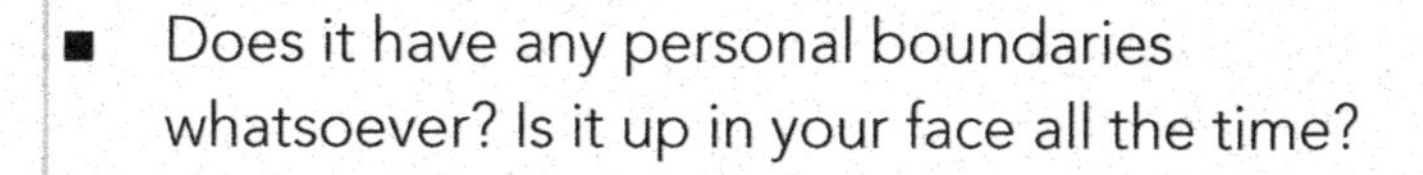

- Does it have any personal boundaries whatsoever? Is it up in your face all the time?

- Does it need your undivided attention? Does it EVER leave you alone?

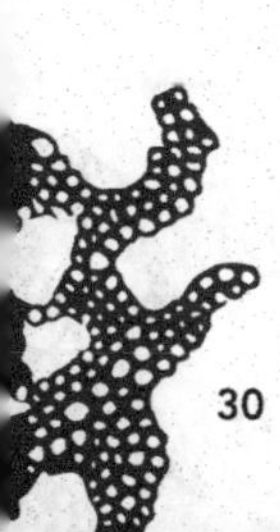

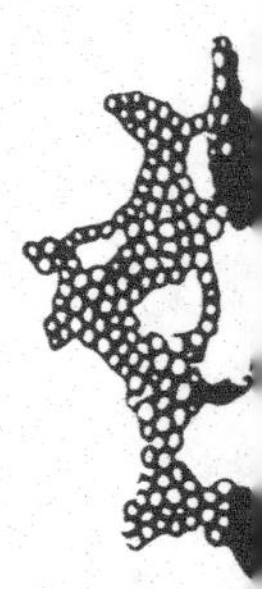

But what's curiosity, really?

Guess what? Curiosity, which you've been practicing in this chapter, is actually an important part of something called *mindfulness*. All 'mindfulness' really means is bringing curiosity to – in other words, paying attention on purpose to – all your experiences. Mindfulness, or present moment awareness, is being curious and noticing each part of our experience, making space and spending time with all five of our senses. It's allowing in our thoughts just as they are (as thoughts, no more) and allowing in our feelings and just observing how they work. We'll return to mindfulness and explore it in more detail in Chapter 3.

If you've done our curiosity exercises, you may notice that your experience of anxiety is a bit more detailed now. Maybe it's richer and more textured. It's like in the example of experiencing the ocean. It was richer and more textured when we asked you to notice all the details. And if you've tried the exercises, you're already doing something different than avoiding your anxiety. Well done! We want you to practice this because that's how we learn and get good at things. We practice them. Below are some suggestions for how you might 'test drive' these ideas when you put down this book – we'll include a section like this at the end of each chapter.

Test drive

Hey, it's time to start noticing context! What we mean by this is that, outside you and inside you, when anxiety shows up, we'd like you to notice what else is happening in your life. We want you to spend time observing beauty, and gratitude, too. Notice when you are visited by longing. Notice ridiculousness. Notice irony. Savor these observations and savor them mindfully. Drink them in as though you are truly thirsty. Can you try that? Cool! See you in the next chapter and we'll talk some more then.

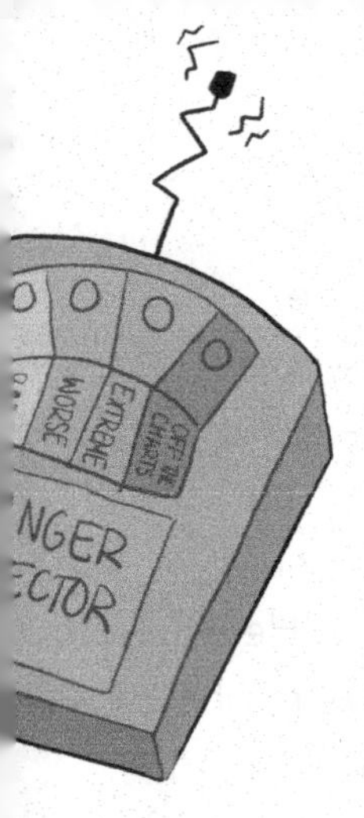

2:

Our minds as threat detectors

Now might be a good time to meet your mind.

You think you know it, but what if you don't? In particular, we're interested in how minds *work*. And this is another area where we can benefit from curiosity. We're going to show your mind to you in a way that may be a bit different to how you're used to looking at it. We want you to be a beginner again here for a moment (like we said in Chapter 1) and pretend that you've just been handed a brain, like a new toy, and you're going to try it out to see how it works.

Have you ever wondered how it is that we humans got to be at the top of the food chain? Compared to our fellow creatures in the animal kingdom we can't run very fast, and we don't really have sharp teeth or claws. It doesn't actually make much sense, does it?

Well, it turns out that we have a secret weapon, in the form of a state-of-the-art threat detection system. That threat detection system is our human brain, and we've traded in all our other weapons for it. The brain is our most powerful weapon, and it's also our most powerful protector. But why? What makes our human brain different from the brains of other animals?

Imagine this: two early humans are hanging out by the mouth of their cave near their newly made fire, which they've just discovered and are totally psyched about. It's night-time, and very dark. The stars are out. Suddenly there's a huge rumbling noise deep in the woods. It sounds like something really big is crashing through the undergrowth. The first human says, "Hey, we better get inside the cave where it's safe! We might get eaten!" The second human says, "Nah, let's just hang out here and chill – or better yet, want to take a stroll in the woods to see what that big sound is?"

Which one of those imaginary humans do you think survived? If you guessed that it was the one who looked for safety in the face of a potential threat, you were right! And you, like us, have descended from a long line of humans who chose safety in the cave rather than exploring the dark forest. Basically, our ability to avoid threat is the result of millions of years of evolution.

So, next time you feel anxious and you aren't sure why, don't beat yourself up. Your brain is simply using an evolutionary survival skill handed down from your ancestors over millennia. Your brain is expressing its evolutionary history. And you're just listening to it!

And your brain, because it has been shaped by all that history, is pretty good at predicting, evaluating, and avoiding threats – both potential and actual ones. This means that our brains help us avoid things that could harm us long before there is any real risk of harm. In other words, a thing doesn't have to *actually* happen for us to learn from it. But how do our brains do that?

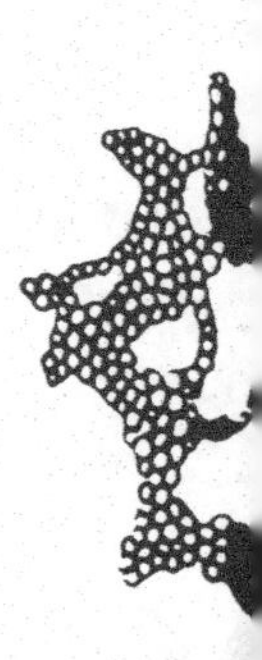

The beginner's guide to your own mind: threat detection basics

Thanks to evolution, we humans have something that other animals don't. That thing is language. And it allows us to do some pretty cool things, like learning about things without experiencing them directly.

Think for a second about how you learn things, like how not to touch a hot pan on the stove. Some people might learn by *actually touching* the hot pan. But that isn't the best way, unless you like getting burned. Another way is for someone to tell you, "Hey, bro, don't touch that. It's hot!" And you learn from them that if you touch it, it will hurt. Right? So that direction, or suggestion, is a rule. And a rule is basically a statement that typically describes a cause-and-effect relationship.

Take for example this proverb: haste makes waste. It means that if you do things quickly, you might not do them well and your efforts could be wasted. This saying is a rule that demonstrates a cause-and-effect relationship – hurrying leads to wasted efforts.

Now, it's your turn! On the next page you'll find some common proverbs. Try to think about them as rules and see if you can figure out what the cause-and-effect relationship might be in each case.

- Practice makes perfect.

- Look before you leap.

- The early bird catches the worm.

We're betting that you could apply each of these sayings to yourself, to guide your actions, without actually having these experiences. In this way, language helps us to learn things without directly experiencing them. Rules, in particular, help us to communicate information quickly, and allow us to cooperate, to predict our future, and to remember and learn from our past.

But what makes language so powerful? To discover more about this, try the next exercise.

Exercise 6: The rabbit and the egg

Let's try something out. We're going to ask you to imagine a few things. Do this at your own pace, without rushing, and as we described in Chapter 1, slow down, step back, and notice your experience as you go, including any thoughts, feelings and physical sensations you have. Ready? Here we go.

Close your eyes and imagine that you're holding a tiny baby rabbit. Imagine you're holding it on your chest, and you can feel how warm it is, feel its heart beating fast (it's a little scared), how light it is, the way its tiny bones move underneath its skin, its little fluffy feet and nails. Imagine how you might hold it, taking care not to squeeze too hard but at the same time being careful it doesn't hop away. Notice how the rabbit smells, how its little nose and whiskers move, how pink its ears are. Imagine that you move slowly to help calm it down.

Write down any thoughts, emotions or physical sensations you noticed here:

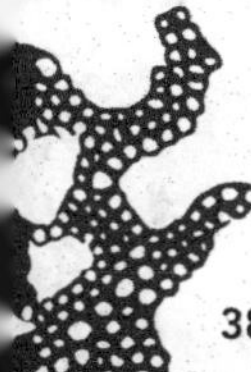

Now imagine you've just cracked open a raw egg from the fridge. Notice that it's cold in your hand, and that the white is a little sticky. Now imagine pouring the raw egg into your mouth and squishing it around with your tongue before you swallow it. Notice that it's cold and slimy.

Write down any thoughts, emotions or physical sensations you noticed here:

If you're like most people, one of those exercises was fun and the other was a bit nasty. Did you notice that, when you slowed down and stepped back, even though there are no actual rabbits or eggs here, you still experienced thoughts, feelings and maybe even some physical sensations? Or, in other words, that you had a psychological experience based on just words in this book and what took place in your imagination? It's pretty mind-blowing that just words – without any actual thing happening – can make us feel so much!

What this means is that our minds have evolved to treat words as literal truths. We can react to them just like the real thing! This is why we like to go to the movies and read books, because when we're using our imagination – or 'languaging brain' – we feel things. We can cheer for a hero or empathize with an underdog. We can feel scared for the teen walking unwittingly into the dark alley where we've predicted that a monster is waiting to get him.

Did you know that the brain experiences social exclusion as physical pain? That's right – the same area of the brain lights up when we experience being socially isolated from our 'herd' as when we experience physical pain. Another way to think about this is that our mind can't tell the difference between an actual physical threat and a verbal, non-physical one.

No wonder our brains are good threat detectors! Right? But they can do even more than that. Your brain can:

- imagine the future
- recap the past
- evaluate
- problem-solve
- speculate
- categorize
- criticize
- judge

All these things let us evaluate threats by predicting what might happen in the future

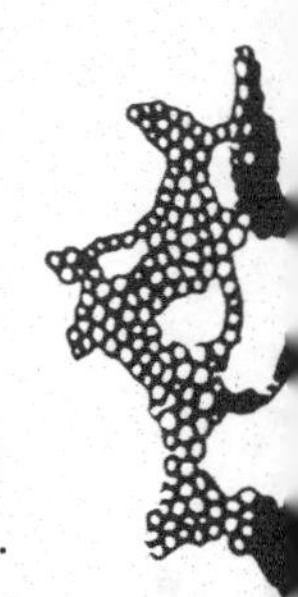

based on the past, and by playing around with how to solve problems – and all from the comfort of a living-room chair, without ever having to take an actual risk. In some ways, your mind is constantly trying to *shut down* curiosity – instead, it just wants you to listen to it, believe it, and get away from whatever it thinks is a threat to you.

Sometimes this is incredibly useful. Sometimes, though, we get stuck in our minds when it's really not necessary or helpful to do so. There are some features of our minds that are helpful to us, but also have a downside.

To understand these features, consider this scenario:

You need to have a new fire alarm installed in your house, and you can pick between two. The first is one that you can turn off whenever you want. The second is on all the time, whether you want it to be on or not, whether you're asleep or awake. Which do you choose?

We're guessing you chose the second fire alarm, because it's probably not a great idea if you can simply turn the alarm off. In order for it to really work well, it would need to be on all the time. And that can be annoying, as anyone who has ever burned toast and had to run around opening windows and fanning smoke away can tell you. Still, it's the safer of the two options.

Minds are like that, too. They're always on, always thinking, and always doing their threat detecting. Have you ever felt down or demoralized because you couldn't turn off those anxious thoughts? If so, well now you know that it's actually not possible for us to turn them off, and that we've evolved like that on purpose.

Exercise 7: Things my mind tells me

Think about times when your mind seems to be on all the time, talking to you. Write down some of the things your mind tells you and the thoughts you have, and also write down the context (time, place, situation) in which these kinds of thoughts tend to crop up.

Thoughts I notice	Time/place/situation
Example: I worry that, when my friends don't text me back or like my social media posts, it means they don't like me.	*Example: At school; if I've had a bad day; if I missed an event due to work and everyone else got to go.*

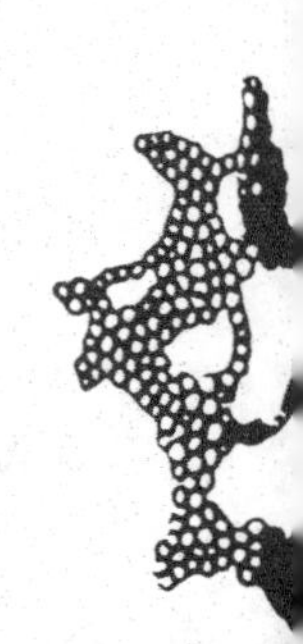

Let's go back to our fire alarm again. So, you have one more choice to make. Again, you get to choose between two alarms. The first one sometimes doesn't go off when there are real fires. The second one goes off a lot, but sometimes when there aren't any real fires – only false alarms. Which one do you think would be safer?

We're guessing that you picked the second option again because it's way more dangerous to have an alarm that doesn't go off when there's a real fire. And, as annoying as false alarms are, the second option is much safer.

Like good fire alarms, sometimes our minds predict threats when there really aren't any. Have you ever felt anxious about something that turned out not to be a big deal? This is just like that.

There's another feature of our minds that can be helpful sometimes, but which also has an occasional downside. Often, we need to make decisions without having all the information we need. This can be tough for our minds. They avoid ambiguity and uncertainty, and as a result they've evolved to be pretty good at filling in the blanks as best they can.

To see what we mean, read the following sentence fragments and write the first word that pops up in your mind:

Mary had a little ________________

Jack and Jill went up the __________________

Who gives a __________________
(haha)

Now let's try something a little more interesting. Do the same with these sentences:

Good students are ____________________

Bad students are ______________________

I am a _____________________

Did you notice how quickly your mind filled in the blanks? You didn't even need to really think about it, did you? Kind of cool to notice. And here's the thing – this kind of mental activity goes on all the time, without us even realizing it.

Context matters, though. Try the next exercise to see what we mean.

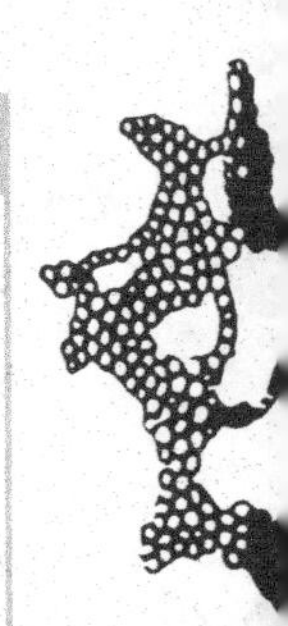

Exercise 8: How does my mind fill in the blanks?

You're at school and a group of kids you know are standing in a huddle, talking. One looks up and sees you, then quickly looks back to the others and laughs. Slow down, step back, and see if you can notice your thinking. What does your mind tell you is happening? Write this below.

You ask your crush to attend a concert with you via text. For a while, there's no response. Then you see that they are typing a response, but taking a while. The three dots that mean they're writing go on... then go off... and then nothing. What does your mind tell you is happening?

You've just finished a science test at school. The teacher says they'll score it in front of you and tell you how you did right away. You hand them your paper and they look at it, furrowing their brow, frowning. What does your mind tell you is happening?

We're guessing that you didn't have any trouble coming up with scenarios about what was going on in each situation. We're also guessing that what you came up with is based on your own particular context. What do we mean by context? This refers to what's going on for you in the moment right now, your past learning history, your mood and your previous experience.

If you struggle with anxiety, we're guessing that your mind came up with some pretty worrying possibilities. Why is that? Well, it's because our minds fill in blanks based on our experiences. This helps us to interpret ambiguous situations and choose what to do next based on those interpretations. The only problem is that our minds aren't always accurate. Remember those ancestors who survived by avoiding danger in the cave? As their descendants, our minds are more likely to imagine the worst and give more importance to things that are threatening or negative than to more positive possibilities. Why? As one of our teachers said:

"You can have lunch many times, but you can only BE lunch once!"

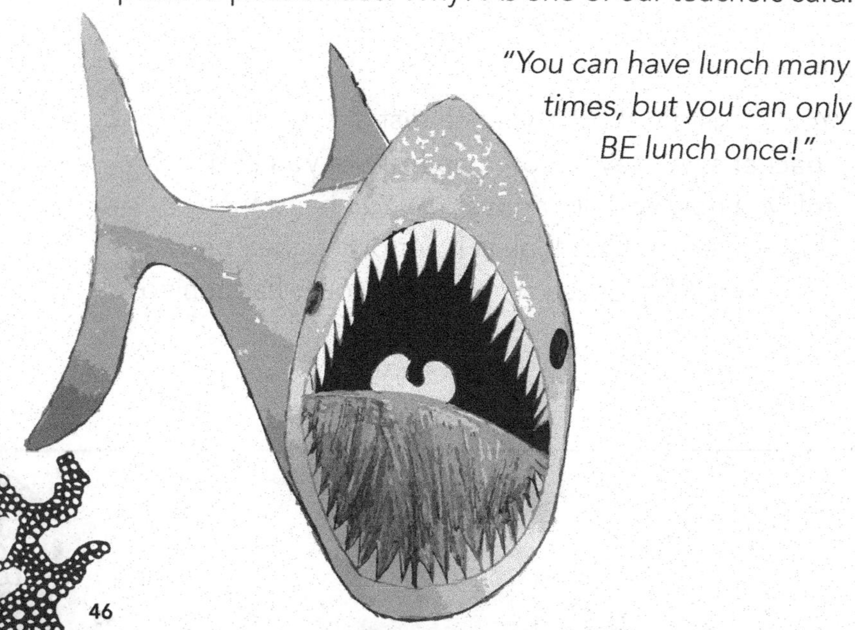

Time travel

There's one more thing that our minds can do that's pretty cool, not to mention essential to our survival: they can time travel! Yep, you heard us right.

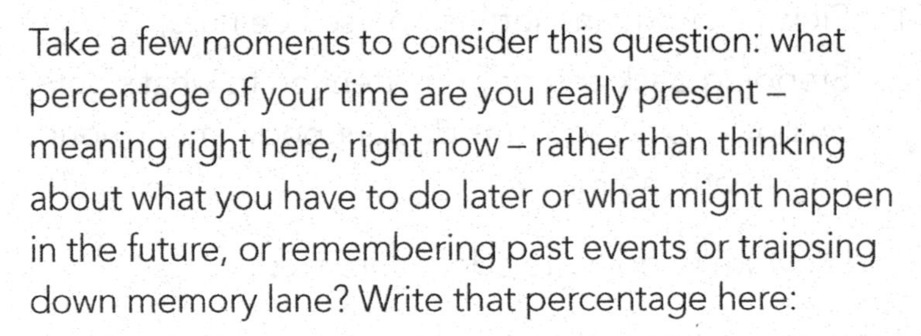

Take a few moments to consider this question: what percentage of your time are you really present – meaning right here, right now – rather than thinking about what you have to do later or what might happen in the future, or remembering past events or traipsing down memory lane? Write that percentage here:

________%

We've asked this question to audiences all over the world in the workshops we run. And you know, most people say they're actually in the present moment only a small percentage of the time.

In other words, *the lights are on, but no-one's home* (meaning present, in the 'here and now') most of the time. Our minds are out in the future, or the past – or they might be sideways, in some imaginary world – trying to help us avoid repeating past mistakes and/or making new ones in the future. This is another mode of threat detection, often driven by anxiety.

The downside, though, is that, if our minds are off gallivanting about in the past or the future, we're not really able to learn from what is going on around us in the here and now. When we're time traveling, we're much less likely to be able to use our skill of *noticing*, which is at the heart of being curious.

What's noticing? Hint hint – you've been learning about the first two steps already:

1. Slowing down and letting yourself be here, now.
2. Stepping back and paying attention to what's going on both inside and outside your body, and in your own heart and mind.

And now we're going to add a third step:

3. Allowing whatever you find to stay in your awareness, without trying to push it away or change it.

Spoiler alert! Noticing is a superpower, and it's incredibly important for helping us find our way through anxiety. Noticing, like curiosity, is part of *mindfulness*. We'll talk more about this in the next chapter. For now, though, you can get started by taking your own noticing skills for a test drive with our simple home practice.

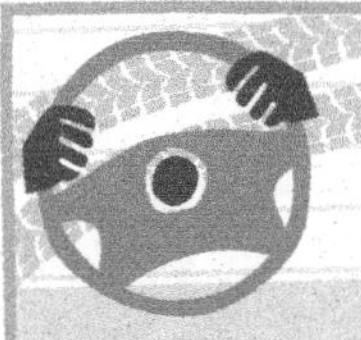

Test drive

This week, we'd like you to just practice your noticing skills some more. When you notice your threat detector going off, see if you can slow down, get curious, and notice on purpose what's happening in your mind, heart and body. Once you've noticed those things, see if you can step back from them. And as you step back, observe that you're able to do just that – to step back and create some distance. Allow whatever experiences you find there to remain, without fighting them or pushing them away. The more you practice stepping back from your thoughts, feelings and actions, the easier it gets to do those things. See you in Chapter 3!

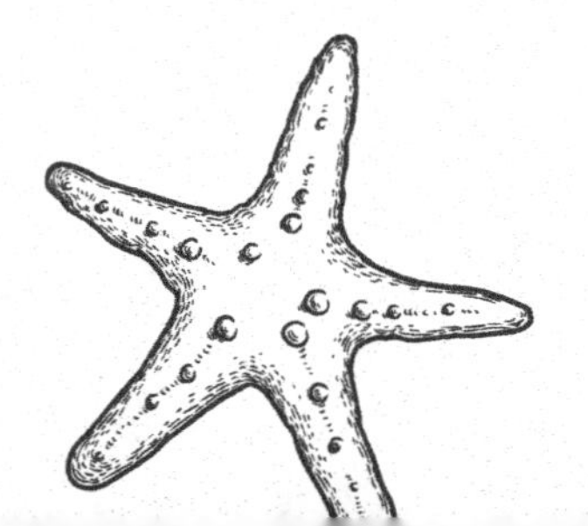

3:

Diving deeper into mindfulness

You know by now that *curiosity* and *noticing* are both part of *mindfulness*. But what exactly is mindfulness and what can it do for you? Why should you practice it? And if you do practice it, how can you use it?

When you hear the word 'mindfulness', what comes into your head? Do you imagine some kind of super-chilled-out yogi sitting and meditating on a mountaintop, all zen, with everything still and quiet? Or maybe you imagine the spin and swirl of thoughts slowly coming to a stop like when someone stops shaking a snow globe? Do you picture being relaxed and calm? Better yet, have you ever tried to be mindful, or to meditate? If so, how did it go? Take a few moments to jot down your general thoughts on mindfulness here.

When we say mindfulness, we don't mean meditating to calm down. In fact, if you've tried to do this, you might have noticed that, well, the struggle is real. Maybe you got distracted, or maybe you felt like it wasn't for you, or that you weren't any good at it. Maybe you noticed your mind pulling you around like a puppy on a leash. Or maybe you got too focused on your bodily sensations and started to get freaked out, your heart beating fast and palms sweating.

But mindfulness really isn't about relaxing, or calming down, even though we do sometimes find stillness through it. Instead, we want you to think about mindfulness in this very simple way:

Mindfulness means being curious, and paying attention, on purpose, to whatever you choose in this present moment.

Simple, right? Paying attention on purpose. It means gently guiding your attention and bringing curiosity to your experience, without defending yourself against it. It's kind of like observing your own experience the way someone might watch sea creatures at an aquarium.

And on that note, just for fun, we invite you to try something...

Exercise 9: An imagined aquarium

Take a few moments to close your eyes and imagine you're standing in the darkened hall of an aquarium. In front of you is a deep blue tank, backlit so the water shimmers a bit. In the tank are jellyfish, sea urchins, fish of all shapes and sizes, eels, sharks and a turtle or two. There are also crabs and snails, even an octopus under a rocky overhang in the reef. Take your time to imagine this. Enjoy the imaginary scene.

Once you've opened your eyes and come back to this book, try to put into words what you were doing in this imaginary experience. See if you can describe how you were paying attention.

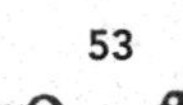

During the aquarium exercise, you may have noticed that you spent a good bit of time, well, noticing. Noticing what you saw, observing from a distance, on the other side of the glass. Perhaps you noticed the colors and movements of the fish, or, if you got really into it, perhaps you heard the hum of the aquarium filter or the sounds of the water?

There are a few other aspects of mindfulness we're wondering if you noticed. If we asked you to notice *when* you were in your mind during this exercise, you probably noticed that you were in the present moment. You probably weren't imagining the next exhibit you might see, or thinking about what you saw earlier in the day. You were just here, just now. This is called *present moment awareness*. And that means exactly what it sounds like: letting your attention stay here, in the present. Renowned horse trainer Warwick Schiller sees it like this: being present means, very simply, that your mind and body are in the same place at the same time.

One more thing we're wondering is if you noticed whether or not you were defending yourself against your experience. Like, have you ever watched a scary movie and noticed that you tensed up, or put your hand to your mouth or hoped that the main character wouldn't get eaten by the monster? If you have, you probably noticed that you were defending yourself against that experience. By that, we mean you were hoping the bad thing in your mind wouldn't come true, or that the feeling of fear and tension would go away. While imagining the aquarium in your mind, you probably didn't defend yourself against it. You simply observed, with curiosity, and let in the experience, without trying to avoid or change it in any way.

So, you're probably thinking two things right now. First, what has this got to do with my life? And second, how come this mindfulness stuff is easier said than done? Seems simple enough to me!

The first question we're going to let roll around for a bit. That's one of those questions that requires actually practicing mindfulness in your daily life to discover. We've tried it on a little bit already in the exercises we've introduced, and we've got lots more to come.

The second question is an important one. It turns out that it's actually *hard* to pay attention on purpose, and to open up to everything going on in our present moment, especially when you feel anxious. It takes practice, for sure! But why is it so tough?

Remember how in Chapter 2 we talked about descending from a long line of humans who capitalized on avoiding threats? Our threat-detecting brain evolved to be on the lookout for threats pretty much all the time. And if you tend towards anxiety? Anxiety amps that up. It *wants* you to pay a lot of attention to possible threats, and it tries its best to keep you focused on them so you don't miss any. If this sounds like you, then try the next exercise to find out more.

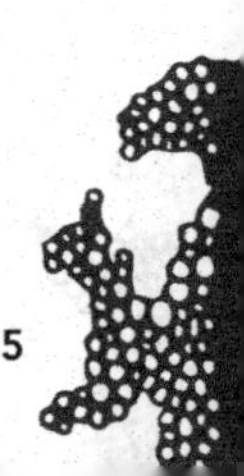

Exercise 10: Sources of anxiety

Take a few moments to jot down some of the thoughts, emotions or physical sensations that put your anxiety on high alert.

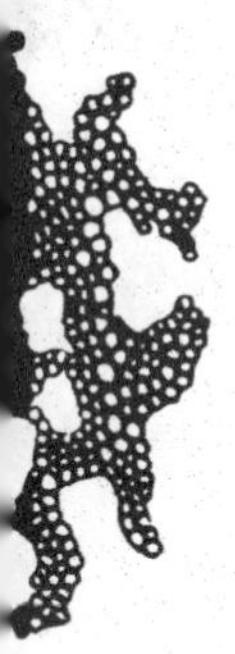

Once you've done this, let's get curious for a few minutes. What do many of the things you've noted down have in common? Does your anxiety tend to notice things that are happening in your *present moment*, or does it tend to pick stuff from the past or things that might happen in the future? Is your anxiety mainly worried about the thoughts, feelings or sensations in and of themselves, or is it more concerned about what those things might *mean*?

You see, anxiety is a good storyteller. It likes to catastrophize about stuff. For example, let's say you have a headache. Anxiety might say quietly (or loudly) *That's probably a brain tumor.* And so you might try to make that fear go away by worrying about it, or researching online, or you might ask for reassurance from parents or doctors.

Or, if you're worried about what other people think of you, your anxiety might say *Those kids are saying you're a fool.* Then you might avoid them, and avoid doing anything remotely foolish. Unfortunately, this is how anxiety tries to protect you from potential threats. It amps up the possible danger to grab your undivided attention and get you to avoid any perceived risks.

The problem here is that anxiety wants you to avoid pretty much everything! And if you spend all your time avoiding things, life can feel pretty small – that's the anxiety cage we talked about in the last chapter. And when you're so stuck, you can't really tell when it makes sense to avoid stuff and when it doesn't.

So, what do you do now? Well, anxiety is going to keep telling its stories. That's what our threat-detecting minds are built to do, as you discovered in Chapter 2. In fact, there are even parts of our brain specifically designed to respond quickly to those stories or to detect those threats. For example, there's this one little part called the *amygdala*. You wouldn't think that such a tiny thing could be important, but it is. The amygdala is basically your brain's alarm system.

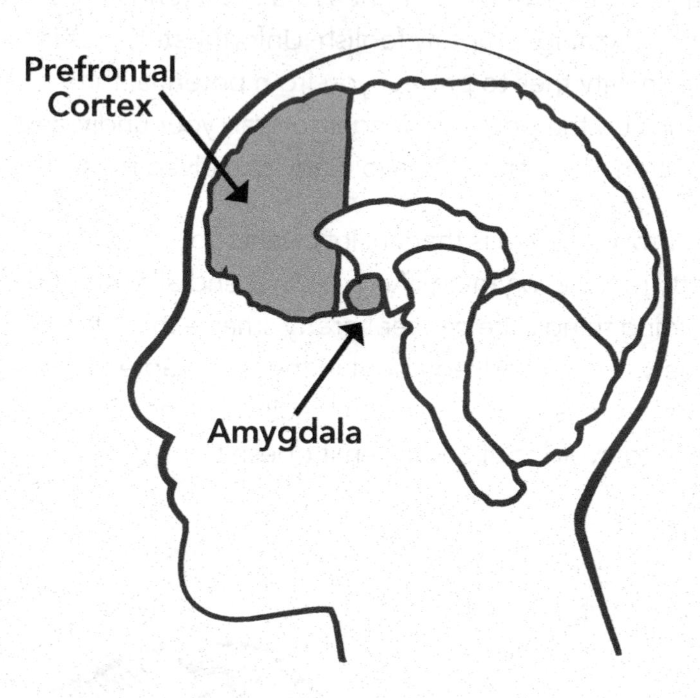

When something starts to signal danger, the amygdala goes on high alert so you can avoid whatever your mind is telling you is a threat, run away from something dangerous or roll over and play dead if that would be more useful. You've probably heard of 'fight or flight' before. Well, when your body goes into that 'fight or flight' response mode, it also basically stops thinking and reasoning so that it can put all its energy into running, fighting, hiding or getting away. In order to do that quickly, when the alarm system gets triggered, the part of your brain that does the thinking and reasoning (the prefrontal cortex, or PFC) actually goes offline or goes to sleep. In other words, none of us think very well or clearly when we're anxious. Instead, we just respond to the alarm signal to which our amygdala is responding.

So hey, this is all really useful if you're actually being chased by a lion or a bear! Unfortunately, it's not all that useful for most other situations. But there is something we can do to help us to get some perspective on when an amygdala response might be helpful and when it might not. On the next pages you will find some things that we can do when our anxiety gets all stirred up.

Three ways to practice mindfulness

First, we can strengthen our ability to notice, be curious, and just hang out, in the present moment. When anxiety feels like it wants ALL our attention, by strengthening our ability to *notice* we can have a greater sense of choice about where we let our focus rest. This isn't about avoiding anxiety or defending ourselves against it. On the contrary, it's about noticing anxiety *and* being curious about other things going on in and around us that might actually be way more important.

To find out what we mean, try the next exercise.

Exercise 11: Mindfulness in action

Is there a craft, puzzle or some kind of art that you like to do? Or do you have a task at home, like washing the dishes, walking the dog or tidying your room? Do you ever just go for a walk? Choose a simple activity of this kind, and practice actively *noticing* while you do it. Notice the movement of your body, the sensations you experience, and what you see, hear, taste or smell. If possible, see if you can notice what you're thinking.

Keep this very simple, maybe just a few seconds or minutes at a time. Let the quality of your attention be gentle, curious and open. See if you can notice little details that are new or unexpected, or that you haven't noticed before. Try to accept all parts of this experience, whether you like and appreciate them or you don't. Remember the imagined aquarium and observe your experience in the present moment, just like you observed those sea creatures.

A second simple way to practice mindfulness is to notice your breath. Simply bring your attention to your experience of breathing, noticing that this goes on all the time, largely outside of your awareness. Notice how your body shifts and changes with each in-breath and out-breath. You might notice your mind tugging you along or distracting you with thoughts. That's normal and to be expected. When you notice this, simply bring your awareness back to your breath. Mindful awareness is an active thing. It shifts and changes.

Exercise 12: Building mindful awareness

If you struggle with anxiety, it can be hard to start practicing mindfulness by focusing on what's going on in your body. So, here's a breakdown of steps you might want to take as part of building up your mindful awareness about anything at all. Focus on:

1. What you can see or hear outside your body.
2. What you can feel on your skin.
3. What you can smell.
4. What you can taste.
5. Your breath.
6. A pleasant experience you remember.
7. A neutral experience you remember.
8. A mildly annoying experience you remember.
9. A sad or frightening experience you remember.

A third way to practice mindfulness is to keep engaged in activities that pull you into the present and keep you there for a while – playing music or sports, doing art, riding horses, or making things with your hands. Stuff where it isn't easy to switch into autopilot and become *mindless*, without paying attention. Pick things where you have to stay focused. In sports, athletes who are mindful tend to have better performance and flow and lower anxiety. In musical performance, more mindful musicians tend to perform better, and in a more connected way with their music.

For people who practice mindfulness frequently, or who meditate regularly, meditation is associated with all sorts of positive changes in the brain including increased connectivity, cortical thickness, and brains appearing 'younger' than in same-aged peers who are non-meditators. That might seem boring or irrelevant to you right now, and we won't overdo it with the details, but it turns out that practicing mindfulness is actually beneficial way beyond just helping people who feel anxious. Mindfulness helps people to be good at lots of things like school and sports and music, and it also improves their general health and wellbeing. Scientists have even measured that in real physical ways in people's brains!

Wow! All that from mindfulness!

Test drive

Practice makes perfect, or at least better! In order to strengthen your skill at being present and noticing, building a practice of mindfulness – even a small one – into your everyday life will be incredibly helpful. Think about something you do every day; something simple, like putting on your shoes or brushing your teeth or eating a meal. Practice noticing whatever that activity is – what it feels like and what you're doing in the moment – and do that activity mindfully. This can be for just a minute or two at a time, to get the hang of paying attention on purpose. See if you can do this a few times a day for a week. It can help to keep a journal of this practice, so that you can write down things you notice about your experience and track changes. Keep in mind that the aim of the exercise is not to not feel anxiety; it's simply to flex and strengthen your ability to pay attention, whether you're anxious or not. Give it a try!

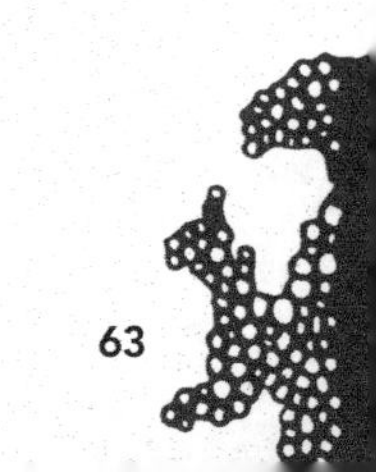

4:

The cost of control and avoidance

After your adventures in mindfulness in the previous chapter, we're sure it isn't lost on you that it tends to be a lot harder to pay attention on purpose to anything other than anxiety during times when we're anxious. That's because our minds perceive anxiety itself as a threat. Like a shark, if you will. And if you were in the ocean swimming and there was a shark, what would you do? You'd try to get the heck out of the water or swim in the opposite direction, right? Your attention would be solely on that shark and your route of escape. That's it.

When you're that scared, everything else shuts down and it's like you're looking at that shark, or your anxiety, through a keyhole. It's all you see. In this way, keeping our attention on our anxiety is, in itself, an attempt to control it so that we can more effectively avoid it. In a sense, our mind treats our experience of anxiety like it's a shark, and our anxiety itself starts to feel toxic and dangerous. And do you know what else? When we look through a keyhole, there's a lot of stuff we *don't* see. We lose touch with what's going on around us. We might even lose touch with ourselves, and our strengths.

Consider a story to understand how this works.

Olivia likes to play soccer. She's been playing for years, and she's pretty good at it. But lately, every time she goes to practice, her mind starts to talk to her. It says things like: "*You're not that good. In fact, you suck at this. Everyone knows. Look, Lily is way better than you. Nobody is really talking to you – they're all talking to each other. They think you're a loser.*"

As those thoughts grow louder, Olivia starts to feel more and more anxious. Her heart pounds. Her stomach is upset, and her hands are sweaty. She has a throbbing headache. So she tries to make herself as small as she can by avoiding her teammates' gaze and standing a little apart so she doesn't have to talk with them. She sits on the bench by herself. When she's asked to go on the field, all she notices is the voice in her head telling her how bad her playing is. She tries to argue with it, and when she does, she misses pass after pass. She thinks: "*If only I weren't so anxious.*" Once the game is over, she gives serious thought to quitting the team, telling herself: "*At least I won't feel so anxious all the time. It'll be a relief.*"

Can you relate to this story? Have you ever thought of giving up something you cared about because of anxiety? Or have you found yourself avoiding experiences so as not to feel anxious? If so, you're not alone. Most of us, at one time or another, have found ourselves in similar situations. And here's the thing: this works. Right? Or does it?

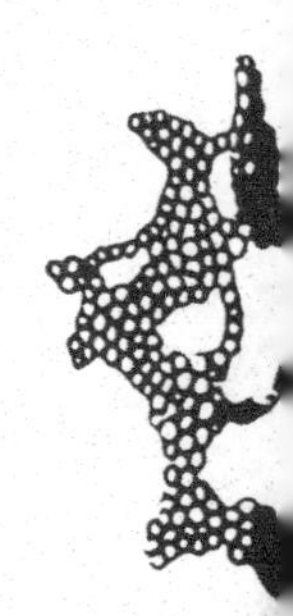

Let's take a look.

When Olivia avoids stuff that makes her feel anxious, she gets some relief. It worked! So, the next time she feels anxious, she does it again. And again. And again. And pretty soon, she gets really good at watching out for her own anxiety, and doing all she can to avoid it.

But then Olivia's life gets really small and cramped. She no longer plays soccer. Her friends drift away. And her short-term fixes are just that: short-term. Her anxiety keeps turning up again, in more and more places. So she has to avoid those places too. Now, in addition to constantly keeping an eye on her anxiety, she feels terrible that she can't make it go away, and she wonders what's wrong with her. Her whole life feels like she's trapped in a tiny room with her anxiety. And it's still demanding her full attention.

Have you ever felt this way? Constantly on edge, just working on not feeling anxious? Again, if you have, you're not alone. This is a very common pattern in most humans. Avoiding threats helped us to survive and evolve, right?

The only problem is that our attempts to avoid anxiety, while they seem to make sense, don't really work even in the way we think they do. Consider Olivia again. She avoids things, and when she does, she gets some short-term relief. But that window of relief gets smaller and smaller, and her focus on anxiety gets bigger and bigger. She spends so much of her time trying to avoid feeling anxious, it captures all her attention.

She loses touch with her experience of who she is – the girl who really likes to play soccer, who is actually pretty good at it. The girl who is a good teammate, who laughs with her friends, who shares their victories and defeats. The girl who is kind and supports her peers, who enjoys running as fast as she can and who sets up killer goals.

Now all Olivia notices is her anxiety. All her attention is on that, and only that. There is no room at all for curiosity and noticing anything else.

Does this resonate with you? Do you have a story like this, in which anxiety soaks up all your attention? What does your struggle with anxiety take away from you? What do you miss most? How much of your day is spent trying to manage, avoid or minimize anxiety? Has your struggle with anxiety cost you, like it has cost Olivia?

Exercise 13: The cost of control

Could there be a cost associated with trying to control your anxiety? See if you can bring your curiosity to bear on that question. Jot down below some things that you wish you had more of in your life. If you weren't working on trying to control your anxiety, what would you want to be doing instead?

What did you notice about this exercise? Was it challenging, or easy? Sometimes we can get so stuck that it actually hurts to think about what we're missing. It can be easy to shut this down, to say it's not for you. Or maybe your anxiety makes it feel impossible. It can be overwhelming. But what if a different life *were* possible? One in which your anxiety wasn't driving from the back seat all the time?

Think about this question: if it were possible to build yourself a life, one that you loved waking up to every morning, would you want that? Your mind might shut this down and tell you it's not possible. But just, for a moment, imagine a world where it *is* possible. Would you want that? And if your answer is yes, then what would you be willing to do to find a way to that life?

Let that question wash over you and we'll come back to it later. For now, you'll need some tools that can help you change your relationship with your anxiety. And the best way to learn these is to try them out.

Here's a crazy idea: What do you think would happen if, instead of running away from the stuff that triggered your anxiety, you ran towards the things that mattered most to you? Instead of avoiding, what if you put together these three steps:

1. Slow down and let yourself be here, now.
2. Step back and pay attention to what's going on both inside and outside your body, and in your own mind and heart.
3. Allow whatever you find to stay in your awareness, without trying to push it away or change it.

...and then added one more step:

4. Turn towards the things your anxiety tells you to run away from.

But wait – why on earth would you do that?!

Let's slow down a bit and see.

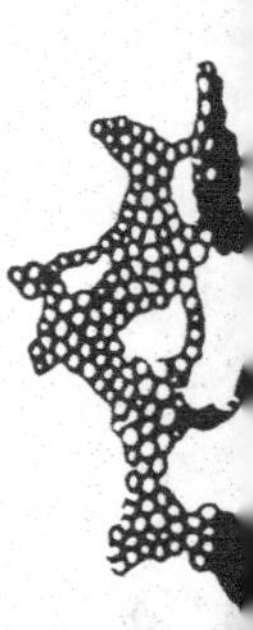

Exercise 14: My anxiety triggers

Take a few moments to write down some places, people or things you tend to avoid because they trigger your anxiety. You can include feelings, thoughts or sensations you avoid, too. We humans tend to avoid anxiety triggers whether they happen inside us or externally.

When you begin to practice slowing down, being curious, noticing and stepping back, you may discover that anxiety tends to show up whenever you do things that feel important.

Why, you ask?

Well, the more you care about something, the more it would hurt to lose it, or to fail to achieve that thing. So anxiety jumps in the way to block the path. Once again, it's your threat-detector mind trying to keep you safe.

In this way, anxiety can actually help you to identify some of the things that you truly care about – because the more you care about a thing, the bigger the anxiety associated with it tends to get.

But if that's the case, then how do you help yourself go after the things you care about? The answer lies in a concept called *willingness*, and we'll talk about this more in the next chapter.

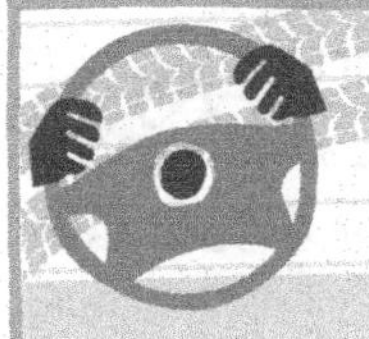

Test drive

As you go through the next week, try to practice the steps we've outlined above. So instead of avoiding the things that make you anxious, try to turn towards them. Before running away, pause. Stay curious. See what you notice – not just what you think and feel, but how the steps are working. If it feels too much to try this out with things that trigger your anxiety, go ahead and try it out with situations that evoke other emotions, either positive or negative. Write down what you learn below. Also, take a little time to consider these questions:

1. What's different about slowing down and noticing rather than avoiding what you're feeling?

2. What feels more effortful – trying to avoid being anxious, or slowing down, getting curious, noticing on purpose and stepping back from your thoughts?

3. When did anxiety most often show up for you? Was it when you were doing stuff that was relatively unimportant, or when you were engaging in activities that had meaning for you?

5:

Befriending your anxiety

Still with us? Great!

By getting this far, you've done some really good work, practiced some really important skills, and asked some really hard questions of yourself about the ways you've been trying to manage your anxiety. Even now, just considering these questions, you're learning. We're sure it still feels scary to imagine slowing down and turning your attention towards your anxiety rather than away from it. But if anxiety jumps in the way every time you try to do things you care about, we're afraid the only way out… is through.

In order to move through your anxiety, it's actually really helpful to make friends with it. And two key ingredients for befriending your anxiety are opening up your awareness and increasing your *willingness.*

Try this mindfulness exercise as a starting point for befriending your anxiety. It's called the 'body scan'. You can read it by yourself and then, after each paragraph, close your eyes and try to imagine it in your mind. Or you can have someone you trust read it to you, or you can listen to Dr Sarah reading it by downloading the recording from the website that we include under the title of each audio track (www.pavpub.com/tired-of-teen-anxiety-resources).

First, get yourself into a nice mindfulness position. By that, we mean upright but not overly rigid, so your breath can flow in and out easily.

Notice the body as a whole. Notice the contact between your body and whatever is supporting you – the chair, floor, bed – whatever you're sitting on. Remind yourself that we're not trying to get anywhere, and we're not trying to achieve any special state. We're just going to try to become aware of what is already here in our bodies. We'll allow things to be exactly as we find them.

Now see if you can let go of the tendency to want things to be a certain way, or to judge how you're doing them. Just follow these instructions as best you can. It's okay if your mind wanders, because that's what minds do. When it does, see if you can gently return your focus to your body.

Notice how your body moves as you breathe. Notice how your chest rises as you inhale and how it lowers as you exhale. Notice as the breath naturally enters the body and leaves the body. And now, gather your attention and move it down the body to your feet. →

Notice the sensations in both of your feet. The sensations in your toes, in the soles of your feet, the tops of your feet. And, if you don't notice any particular sensations there that's fine, just be aware of that. Or maybe the sensations are very subtle. This is your experience right now, and there is no wrong way to do this. We're simply observing your experience as it unfolds.

Now take a deep breath in and shift your attention to your ankles. What sensations do you notice here? The joints, the inside, the outside and all around them? What is here in your ankles right now?

On your next out-breath, shift your attention to your lower legs. Notice any sensation with what they are in contact with. And again, notice also if there are no sensations and remember that whatever you experience, it's perfectly fine.

On the next in-breath, move your attention from your lower legs to your knees. Just focus on them right here, right now. Notice any sensations or lack of sensations in them as you breathe.

With the next out-breath, move your attention to your thighs. The sensation of contact with clothes on the surface of your skin, maybe a heaviness or a lightness. Notice any sensation or lack of sensations. Continue to focus on your thighs.

Now, when you're ready, on your next in-breath, notice your whole body as you breathe. Imagine

what it would be like if the breath came through your whole body. Imagine that your entire body is porous – full of tiny holes in your skin (which it actually is!). Just notice this for a few moments.

On your next out-breath, bring your attention away from your legs and your whole body and focus just on your hips. Imagine your breath flowing into this region and notice any sensations that might arise. Breathe into your hips deeply.

On your next out-breath, bring your attention to your back. Start with your lower back, moving all the way up to your shoulder blades until you're aware of the whole of your back. Inhale, noticing any sensations as they come and go.

On the next out-breath, bring your attention to the front of your body. See what sensations are there as you breathe in and out. From time to time, you'll notice yourself getting distracted or bored or maybe hoping that this will hurry up. That's okay. Nothing has gone wrong. Just notice this. And then, without judgment, gently bring your attention back to your body.

Next, bring your attention to your lungs, breathing in and breathing out. Take a deeper and more intentional breath, and shift your attention to your hands and your eyes. Be aware of both your hands and your eyes at the same time. Is there warmness, a tightness, or do you notice any sensations at all? What is here in your body at this moment? →

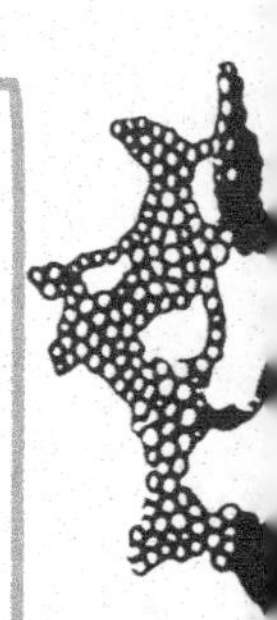

On the out-breath, shift your attention to your shoulders and neck. What sensations can you feel here? Whatever they are, just notice them. Remind yourself that you don't have to control anything. Just observe and notice them, the way you might notice waves in an ocean or shells on a shore. We appreciate, admire and explore. We can't always control or fully understand.

On the next out-breath, move your attention to your head and face. Your jaw, your lips, your nostrils, your nose, your cheeks and the sides of your face. Your ears, eyes and eyelids, your eyebrows and the space between them, your forehead and temples, and your scalp. Imagine your breath can fill your whole head and refresh each and every part of your face with each and every in-breath.

Now imagine that the breath can fill your entire body as you breathe. Filling your whole body as you breathe in and leaving it as you breathe out.

Allow yourself to be just as you are. And acknowledge that you've done this. Even if it seems unusual. Notice this. Notice your body as a whole as you continue to inhale… and… exhale. Allow your body to be as it is. Feel a sense of coming home to your own body. Remind yourself that this process is available to you at any time of your life, unfolds from moment to moment and day to day.

When you're ready, and at your own pace, return your attention to the room that you're sitting in.

When you did this exercise, what did you notice? What did you learn?

And did you notice the part of you that was doing all this observing and learning? Perhaps you noticed a little bit of distance between this 'observing you' and your anxiety. Maybe you found a little more breathing room, or maybe, just for a bit, your anxiety felt somewhat less overwhelming or all-encompassing. If so, you've started to find your way to the 'still point' – the quiet place inside you where you can step back and observe your anxiety on purpose as simply one of your experiences, with a little distance and detachment. So even if anxiety or worry is swirling all around you, you can step back and observe – sort of like watching a storm without getting sucked up into it.

If you cultivate this way of observing your anxiety, you'll get better and better at finding your still point. And there are two key steps that will help.

Step 1: Open up your awareness

First, let's start with the idea that there are different ways to pay attention on purpose. You can pay attention to something to avoid it. You can also pay attention to something with curiosity and openness. One of these ways of observing is helpful, and the other? Not so much. Let's unpack this a little.

Remember our discussion in Chapter 4 about how you might pay attention to a shark if you were swimming in the ocean? Try the following exercise, to help you understand how we can pay attention in different ways.

Exercise 15: Sharks and kittens

If you were swimming alongside a big, dangerous-looking shark:

- What would you notice?

- What would you pay no attention to whatsoever?

→

- What would the purpose of your noticing be?

- How urgent would your noticing feel?

- Would the scope of your awareness be broad, where you noticed lots of things around and about the shark, or narrow, where you focused only on the shark?

→

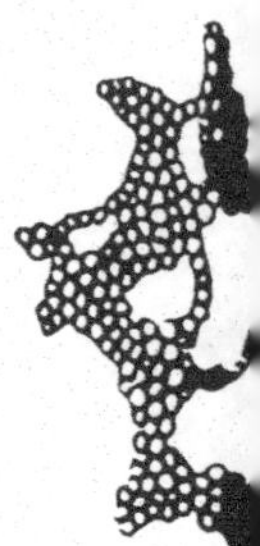

Now, try something a little different. Imagine for a moment, in as much detail as you can, a really squirmy, very cute kitten. Think about these next few questions:

- What would you notice?

- What would the purpose of your noticing be? Would it be different than when you noticed the shark?

- Would it feel urgent, in the same way that you might notice a shark?

- Would the scope of your awareness be broad, where you noticed lots of things around and about the kitten, or narrow, where you focused only on the kitten?

Assuming you aren't scared of kittens, you probably noticed that the quality of your attention on it versus the shark was pretty different. Perhaps it was gentler, perhaps you noticed more things. And the purpose of your attention was probably very different – maybe you wanted to befriend, to invite, to show kindness, to appreciate the kitten. Also? Even if that little squirmball nibbles or scratches you a bit, you might be more willing to allow that – to notice it, and to stick around anyway, basking in the cuteness.

Making a distinction between these two really different qualities of awareness is important to how you relate to your anxiety. One (noticing the shark) is about control. The other (noticing the kitten) is about fully engaging, being curious, and making space.

Step 2: Increasing willingness

The second key step in finding your way to your still point is called *willingness.*

What's willingness, you ask? Well, lots of people think they can overcome their anxiety with willpower. They might think *"I should be able to suck it up and just get on with things"*, or *"I'll grit my teeth and get through it."*

Willpower is overrated, and it can actually be counterproductive. Really, willpower is just beating yourself up so you can do a hard thing. For some of us, sometimes, in short bursts, it works. But as a general long-term strategy, it's a real downer.

You see, there's a much less effortful and much more effective way to help yourself face your fears – willingness. Let's do an imagination exercise to help explain what we mean.

Exercise 16: Bug munching

Pretend, for a moment, that someone is standing in front of you holding a big brown insect, about the size of a blackberry. Imagine that they hold it out to you in their hand, and they dare you to eat it. What would you say?

Write your answer below and rate your willingness to eat the insect on a scale of 1-10, with 1 being "No way!" and 10 being "Okay, sure!" Here we go.

A stranger holds out an insect. Will you eat it?

Your answer:
Willingness level:

The stranger holds out the insect again, but this time they offer you twenty dollars to eat it. Will you eat it?

Your answer:
Willingness level:

The stranger points out that you haven't eaten anything in three days, and you are starving. They offer the insect again. Will you eat it?

Your answer:
Willingness level:

The stranger tells you that they are a doctor, shows a legitimate medical license, and tells you that this insect has life-saving properties and will ensure

that you are healthy, fit and active forever (pretend you believe them). Will you eat it?

Your answer:
Willingness level:

The stranger has you think about someone you really love, and tells you that by eating this insect, you will save that person from eating twenty more just like it. Will you eat it?

Your answer:
Willingness level:

Pretty silly exercise. But perhaps you noticed that your willingness level changed somewhat as you went through it. We're guessing that eating the insect was never something you were terribly excited about. Still, you may have noticed your willingness increase slightly as the conditions around eating the insect changed. And maybe, just maybe, how you thought and felt about eating that insect changed a little too.

It works in a similar way with anxiety. If you choose to crank up your willingness, it changes your experience of your anxiety. To play around with this idea in real life, have a go at the next exercise.

Exercise 17: Willingness in the wild

Try out the following activities to see willingness at work in your everyday life.

- When it's raining, choose to go outside without a raincoat. Let yourself feel the rain, turn your face to the sky, notice the drops falling on you.
- While you're waiting in a long, boring line, say to yourself, "Okay." Let yourself relax. Explore what it feels like to wait in line, and don't fight it.
- If you're eating your favorite chocolate bar, and you have only one bite left, give it away. Notice what it feels like to do this.
- Try a new food you aren't accustomed to. Be curious about how it tastes, and notice how your body responds. Look for things you didn't expect about it.
- Switch your right and left shoes and, very carefully, walk around for a short distance. See how that feels. Notice what's different about this and wearing your shoes on the usual feet.
- Give someone a compliment. Make eye contact if that feels right for you, and tell them something you like or admire about them. Watch how they respond, and notice how you feel.

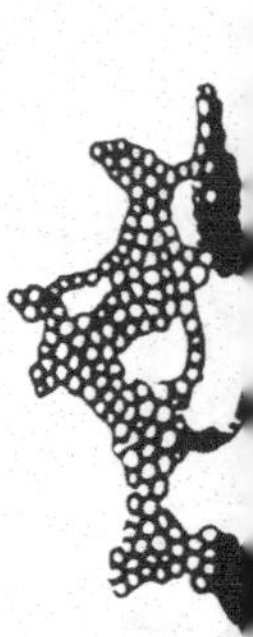

Putting awareness and willingness together

So, the two steps to finding your 'still point' are:

1. Opening up your awareness, gently, with curiosity, even when things feel hard or scary; and
2. Cranking up your willingness to experience whatever it is you are noticing.

When you start to practice these two steps in turning towards your anxiety, things will begin to feel quite different for you. These two small steps add up, and together they will help you find your way to your still point – a place where you can feel and experience your anxiety while still being grounded. It does take time and practice, though. To find out how this works with anxiety, or any other unpleasant or unwanted thought or emotion or sensation, try the following audio track.

Take a few moments to settle in someplace comfortable that's quiet, where you can be by yourself for maybe ten or fifteen minutes. Let yourself settle in slowly, noticing each breath. As you breathe out, see if you can let your body settle a little bit more fully. Take your time, there's no rush. If your mind is all aswirl, that's fine. That's what minds do. Just give a little mental nod to whatever might be swirling about, and when you can, bring your attention back to your breathing. →

If you're willing, see if you can call to mind a specific situation when you felt anxious. Imagine you could watch yourself like you were on a movie screen, seeing what was going on around you, and seeing yourself in that moment. See if you can make space for whatever thoughts and feelings arise as you do this, without trying to change them. Remember to be curious, and notice how those thoughts inhabit your body. And slow down and explore the thoughts you're having. Invite them to come visit, and do whatever they wish, and leave whenever they're ready.

Take special care to notice your anxiety. Make a big space for it, to notice it gently, with openness and curiosity. If it had a shape, what would it look like? Feel like? Could you eat it? I mean what it is REALLY like? Does it have a smell or a texture? Try to notice every single detail. Muster up everything you possibly can.

Spend a few moments simply doing this, perhaps two or three minutes. Remember to stay in touch with the part of you that is choosing to notice and making space for this experience.

[pause]

As you're noticing, notice that your anxiety is an experience you're having. Notice the part of you that is observing… and that in this observing part of you, there is a still point. This is a quiet place from which you can observe your experience… where you can create space for it… where you can choose to allow →

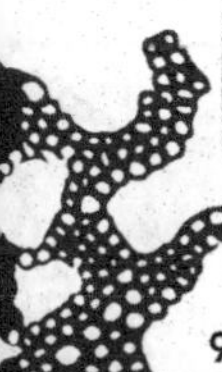

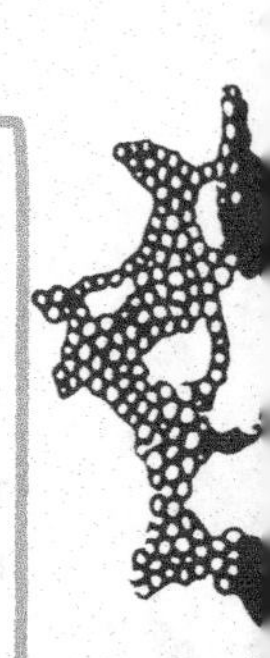

it to come and go... and choose to give up trying to control it. Notice that in this observing part of you, you have all the space you need for any emotions at all, no matter what size those emotions are, and that includes anxiety. In this space, there's you and then there's your experience. You're vast enough to contain all of it. In this observing space, everything you feel is okay.

[pause]

When you're ready, connect back with your breathing, and open your eyes. Feel free to jot down below any reactions to or thoughts about this exercise, what you have noticed, and anything you might have learned.

All great journeys begin one step at a time, one foot in front of the other. It helps if, on your journey, you are moving towards something that matters so much to you that it makes facing your anxiety worth it. In the next chapter, we'll discuss a powerful tool that will help you to really dial up your willingness.

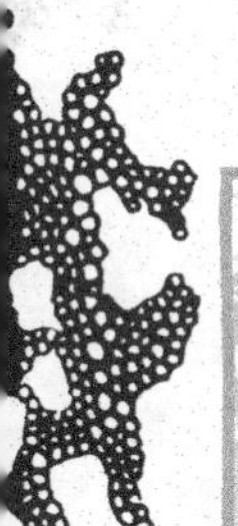

Test drive

This week, we encourage you to begin your willingness practice throughout your day. Take time to notice stuff that you're avoiding or protecting yourself from in some way. Then see if you can first slow down and open up to let the experience in, then crank up your willingness and turn towards that experience rather than turning away.

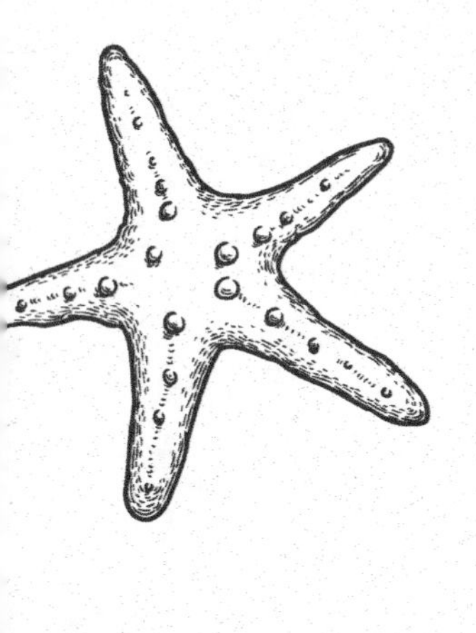

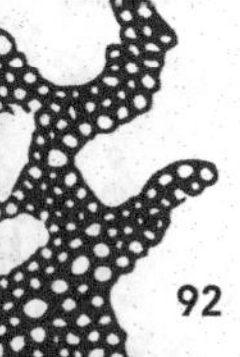

6:

Values – what you care about

In the previous chapter, you learned about willingness and began to practice it out in the world. This probably feels very different to when you were trying to control and avoid your anxiety. When you slow down and make space for what you're feeling, you start to learn from those feelings. But why do we even have feelings? Like, what's their purpose?

Well, we've already discussed how anxiety is a form of information – it tries to keep us safe by alerting us to possible threats – and our emotions give us information too. They help us notice different aspects of our experiences so we can respond effectively to them. But it's hard to get that particular information if we're busy avoiding all the emotions we'd rather not feel. Instead of learning from them, we just feel pushed around by them. And the more we try to avoid them, the bigger and more insistent these things get!

What if, instead of avoiding what you're feeling, you let yourself experience it, just as we played around with in Chapter 5? What if, in order to discover what they have to offer, it's important *not* to manage or avoid thoughts and feelings? What if you could learn something really valuable? And this might sound a bit crazy, but what if the biggest, scariest emotions are actually our best teachers? Like, what if they teach us about what's most important to us in life? And maybe they're shouting loudly because it's really important to pay attention to teachers… well, most of them anyway.

What if sometimes scary, hard or unpleasant thoughts and feelings are the very things that connect us to each other? What if everyone, every single person, had their own unique worries and fears that they, too, struggled with? That they, too, were scared to think about or share with anyone else? Wouldn't that be interesting?

See if you can let yourself imagine that for just a moment (even though your mind is probably telling you that this isn't the case – thanks, mind!).

And what would that be like – the idea that those things that make us feel the most alone are exactly the same things we all share? What would that mean for your heart? Would it mean that your heart could rest? Take a few moments to listen to your heart right now. See if you can notice, and make space for, what it wants, what it wishes for, what it longs for.

In fact, let's do a little exercise in which we listen very carefully to our hearts. We've all probably been listening very carefully to our brains, but let's slow down and listen to our hearts too. If you like, you can have someone you trust read this next short section for you. Or you can listen to the recorded version of it, or you can read it quietly to yourself then close your eyes and try to think back over the questions asked.

Audio track

www.pavpub.com/tired-of-teen-anxiety-resources

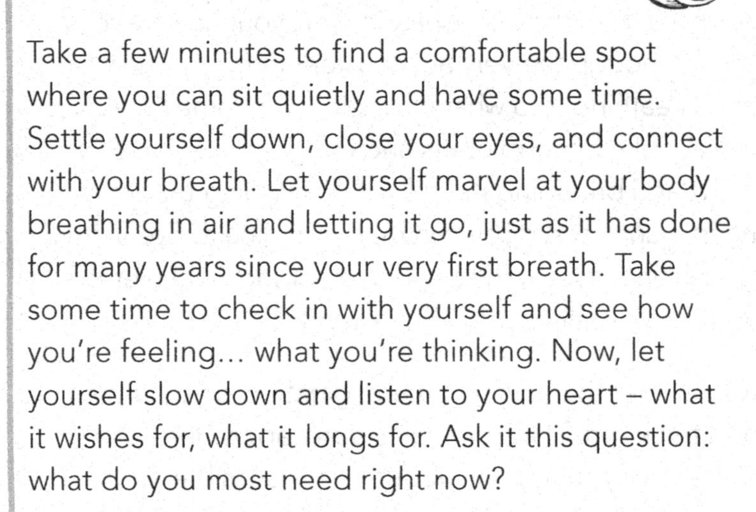

Take a few minutes to find a comfortable spot where you can sit quietly and have some time. Settle yourself down, close your eyes, and connect with your breath. Let yourself marvel at your body breathing in air and letting it go, just as it has done for many years since your very first breath. Take some time to check in with yourself and see how you're feeling… what you're thinking. Now, let yourself slow down and listen to your heart – what it wishes for, what it longs for. Ask it this question: what do you most need right now?

Imagine that you can create life – your life – as though you are an author, and your life is the story you will write. What kind of story would you write? What do you want to move towards in your life?

Think about the stuff you struggle with when you're anxious. Has the struggle got in the way of building that life you imagine? What do you want back? What does your heart say about that?

Let's unpack this idea, like you might unpack a suitcase. See if you can bring to it that gentle, curious, open quality of attention you practiced earlier.

What's in that suitcase?

→

Take a few minutes now and listen to what your heart is saying. What does your heart want most? It's okay for your heart to ask for whatever that is.

And now breathe into whatever it is your heart is asking for. As though the very act of listening to your heart, and breathing into what it asks for, can somehow make it real. Take a few minutes and imagine listening to your heart and breathing in and out. Each thing that your heart wants, see if you can really imagine it. Every little detail. See if you can see yourself doing whatever it is your heart really wants. Whatever it is.

Remember that this is your imagination, so go ahead and think big. The usual rules don't apply here. We're not asking you to think about what's possible, we're asking you what your heart wants. See if you can see yourself not being scared, or being scared but doing what's important anyway, like talking to people you might want to be friends with, or trying out for the football team, or singing a solo in the play – whatever it is that your heart wants. Just breathe it in. A few more times now, that's it. Keep going. Breathe in and out. In and out. In and out. Until you've filled up your lungs with everything that your heart wanted. Keep going. A few more breaths, that's it. In and out. Nice.

Then slowly, and when you're ready, because there's no rush, slowly start to bring yourself back to the room you're in. Notice the chair holding you. Notice the floor below you. Notice any smells that are present. Notice the temperature of the air. And, finally, open your eyes, have a good stretch, and come back fully to the room.

When you try to control or squash down one part of your experience, like your anxiety, you may notice that all the other hues and aspects of your experience – the joy, the longing, the wishing, the happiness – are squashed down and dulled too. So see if you can keep practicing expanding your awareness to all the different aspects of your experience – the parts you don't like as well as the parts you do – gently, kindly, and with openness and curiosity. This will open up another doorway for you – a doorway that leads to a sense of meaning and purpose, and to something that brings you a feeling of 'aliveness' and vitality. A doorway to something we call 'valuing'.

So what exactly is 'valuing'?

First of all, it's an active verb. It's not just thinking about something – it's *doing*. A value is something that really matters to you – something that, when you do things that are related to it – gives you a sense of vitality, meaning and purpose. It might be a characteristic that you want to embody, like kindness, bravery or learning well. And you can have more than one value, in different areas of your life! For example, you might want to be a great friend when you're with your pals, a good role model when you're babysitting, and a fierce competitor if you're playing a sport you love.

Values are personal – they're yours and yours alone, and they aren't influenced by anyone else. You choose them for yourself, freely. And you know what else? In any given moment of any day, they're accessible to you. No matter what!

Think about it like this: if connecting with people is a value, how might you embody that? How might you embody it at the park? How might you embody it at school? By yourself at home in your room? While you are eating breakfast? So long as you keep your value in mind, you can choose it as a compass to orient what you do, and how you are, at any given moment.

Sometimes young people aren't quite sure what their own values are – and that's completely fine and normal! It simply means you're on the road to discovering what they are.

Let's explore that a bit.

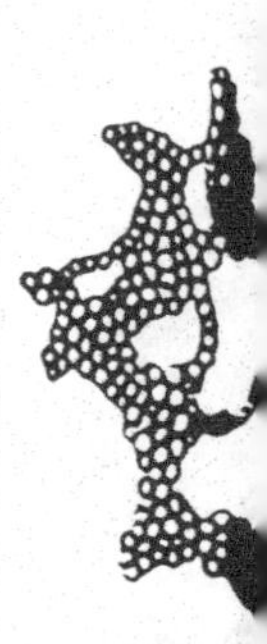

Exercise 18: Mission to Mars

Imagine for a moment that a scientist at an international space exploration collaborative has created a rocket that can successfully fly people to Mars. On Mars, they've built an amazing human habitat that has everything required to sustain life. This habitat has food, water, heat and light; all the things you'd need to survive.

There has been a lottery, and YOU have won a ticket to go on the rocket to Mars! And you decide to go, you bold adventurer, you! However, there's a catch. Well, three catches to be exact. First, you can't take anyone with you. Second, you can never come back to Earth, ever. And third, you have to leave in just twenty-four hours.

We suggest you take a few minutes on your own to imagine this scenario. Really get yourself into it, with your head and your heart too. Then answer the following questions:

If you found this out right now, how would you spend the next twenty-four hours before boarding the rocket? Who'd be with you? And what would you do?

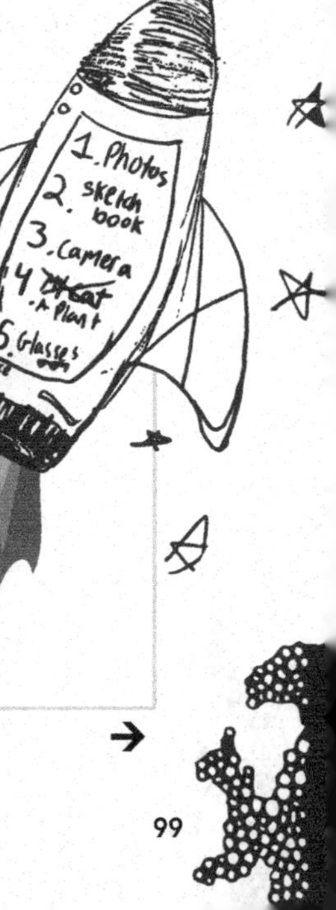

→

- Now imagine that you can only bring five personal items with you. These should be reminders of the life you've known, and they should also summarize the person you've been on Earth and/or the person you most want to be on Mars. What will you bring?

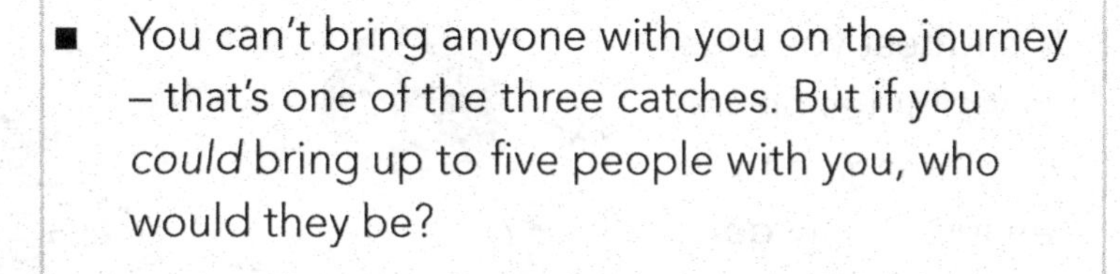

- You can't bring anyone with you on the journey – that's one of the three catches. But if you *could* bring up to five people with you, who would they be?

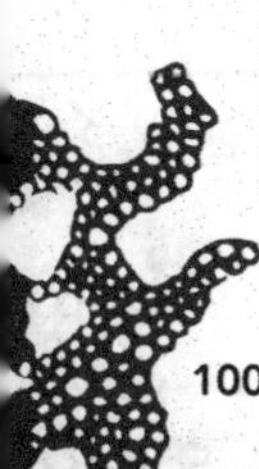

As we discussed earlier, when you get caught up in trying to get rid of anxiety, you tend to lose touch with the things that really matter to you (i.e., the stuff in your heart). Has this happened to you? Take a few moments to remember the last time you focused on the things and people you wrote about in the exercise above. Has it been a while? Or, asked another way, what do you spend more time on during your day – working on your anxiety, or working on things that feel really important and spending time with the people you really love?

While you let your attention rest on the pursuits, activities, and people you care about, see if you can slow down and notice what's going on in your heart. Whatever you're feeling there, do you notice a sense of importance when these things come to mind? Take your time. And if your anxiety is loud, simply notice that and zoom into your heart. See what's in there.

The things that truly matter to us – those things that give us a sense of meaning and purpose – these are what we call *values*. A value is a bit like a lighthouse – it gives us something to head towards if we're caught in a storm. It's a beacon to connect with and follow. It can provide a guiding star for your life, for the things you choose to do, and for the people with whom you spend your time.

What is you aren't sure what your values are? How do you know, or find out, what you value and hold dear? As a teen, this may be a time in your life when you're just beginning to discover your values, and this process is something that will continue throughout your whole life. You might have some ideas about what those values are, or you might not yet be clear about that. Wherever you are on your valuing path, we encourage you to keep walking, and to keep discovering, even if that path isn't always 100% clear. You see, valuing is all about the journey rather than the destination. It's kind of like the novelist E L Doctorow said about writing:

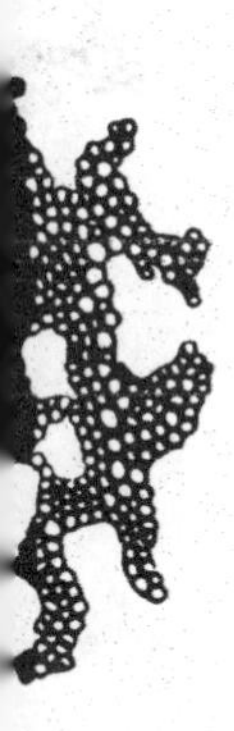

"Writing a novel is like driving at night. You can only see as far as the headlights, but you can make the whole trip that way."

So, dear author of your own story, what will the novel of your life be? How about we share an exercise with you where you can explore this a bit?

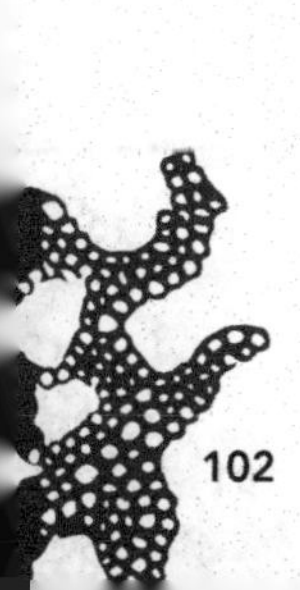

Exercise 19: Who I want to be

Imagine that you're writing a novel with a really cool main character. This is an individual you really admire – someone you'd be totally fascinated by and want to read more about. It's someone who would hold your interest and inspire you. The character can be based on someone you know or a celebrity, or they can be someone you just made up in your head.

Once you have that character in mind, please answer the following questions:

- What adjectives would you use to describe their personality or other characteristics? Take your time and see if you can come up with 8-10 adjectives.

- Now imagine that you have to get rid of all but three of these adjectives. Which ones will you keep? Choose the three that you most aspire to embody yourself.

- What are some ways in which you could embody these characteristics? What are some things that you could do as steps towards achieving that?

- When you embody these characteristics, what effect does this have on you? What do you notice?

- When you embody these characteristics, what are the effects on the people around you? Reflect on this for a few minutes before writing down your thoughts.

- What is one thing that you could do every day to embody these characteristics?

How did you feel while doing this exercise? Did you notice feeling uplifted? Maybe you noticed anxiety jumping in the way. You can decide, at any given moment, which direction to go in – to listen to anxiety or to follow your values. As the writer Anaïs Nin famously said: "*Life expands in proportion to one's courage.*" And the root of the word 'courage' is the French word *coeur*, meaning 'heart'. So the word courage literally means 'following your heart'.

Following your heart can often mean running headlong into anxiety. So the question then arises, now what? You have a choice to make: either you can keep moving in the direction of what you care about, or you can take a hard swerve off course and away from anxiety. It can help to ask yourself this question: do you want your life to be about trying not to be anxious, or do you want it to be about the stuff that really matters to you?

Now, you might say, "*Well, first I need to get rid of my anxiety, and THEN I'll pursue my values.*" But think about it – how has that worked out for you so far? Take a few moments to reflect again on the efforts you've made to get rid of your anxiety, and whether they succeeded in the short- and long-term.

You may have noticed that, no matter what you do, anxiety tends to stick around. Especially if you fight with it. It demands your undivided attention and, if you give in to that, you have very little bandwidth left to do the things you truly care about and follow your values.

Everyone's experience is different. As a teen, maybe you feel pushed around by wanting to fit in and do the stuff others do. Maybe you feel pushed around by wanting to belong. Maybe you feel constrained by stories from your past about what might be possible for you.

To give you some more ideas about values and valuing, try the next exercise.

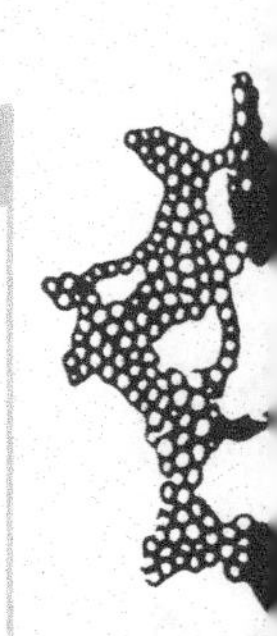

Exercise 20: Identifying values

Below is a menu of common values. We want you to put an X beside the things that seem important to you in your life right now. If you want, in the blank spaces at the end you can also add extra ones we haven't mentioned that are important to you.

Being a good friend	
Caring for my family	
Being a good student	
Being athletic	
Having a sense of humour	
Being a good person	
Seeking wisdom	
Being kind	
Sharing	
Being free	
Being responsible	
Being fair	
Telling the truth	

→

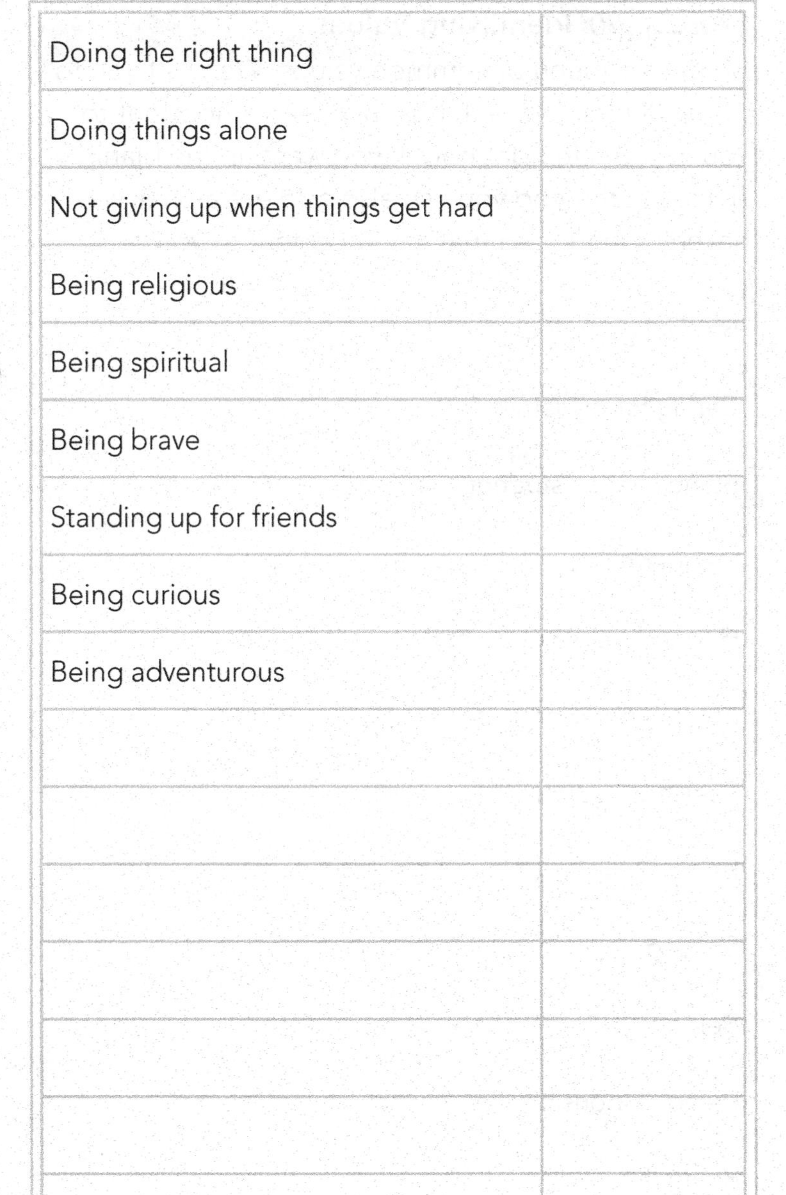

Doing the right thing	
Doing things alone	
Not giving up when things get hard	
Being religious	
Being spiritual	
Being brave	
Standing up for friends	
Being curious	
Being adventurous	

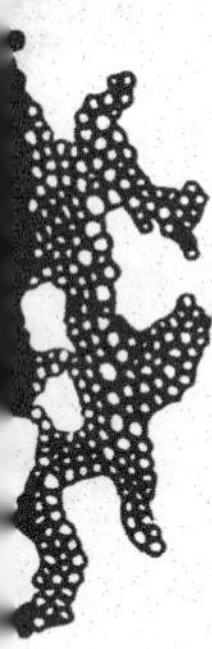

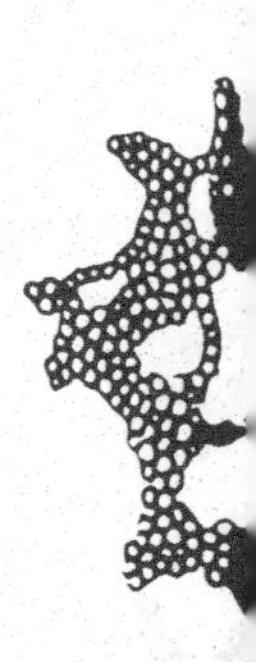

It's helpful to know that what you value might vary depending on the situation you find yourself in. Context matters. Also, you choose your values freely – valuing isn't about 'shoulds' or 'have tos' imposed by anyone else. People can sometimes get really rigid about values, and the way they think about them can move from 'stuff that feels important' to 'stuff I must do' – to the point that they may actually feel oppressed by them.

Test drive

This week, we'd like you to think about the stuff you really care about. Some of that will be what you wrote down earlier in this chapter, and some will be what you imagined when we asked you to close your eyes and think about what your heart wanted most. The next thing we want you to notice is the stuff that gets in the way of you doing more of what you care about. You can write some notes below. Again, this is a noticing exercise, but this time we'd also like you to write down the stuff you care about and what gets in the way of you doing more of it. Once you have a clearer idea of what gets in the way, you'll have more information and more choices about how you go forward or what you do next.

The stuff I care about	The stuff that gets in the way of me doing what I care about

→

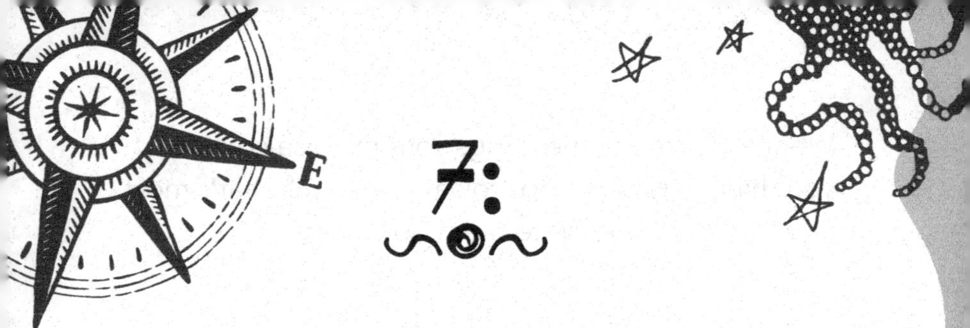

7:

Building a values compass

We've spent a lot of time imagining our values, and reflecting on times when we aligned our actions with the things that we care about – and when we didn't. If you did the exercises in Chapter 6, you'll have started to notice thoughts and feelings that get in the way when you try to move towards your values. Now we'll take a deeper dive into what's important and valuable to you, and see what happens when the rubber hits the road.

Sometimes you've lived with anxiety so long that you might not know where it ends and you begin. When this happens, sometimes it's hard to find what you care about. It can be easier to figure this out by *doing* stuff rather than *thinking* about it. We call trying things out to see how they work 'discovering'. And discovery often occurs outside your comfort zone. In fact, being in your discovery zone and feeling uncomfortable or anxious while trying something new means you're learning!

Our anxious minds often throw themselves in our path when we engage in discovery and do things that connect with our values. They might say unhelpful things like, "*We can't do this*" or "*This is too scary*".

What are some of the things your mind says when you think of taking steps towards the stuff that's most important to you? Write them down here.

If you wrote down stuff like "But I can't" or "It's too hard", or "I'll never be able to...", you aren't alone. But here's the question: are you going to let anxiety determine what direction you go in your life? Or will you choose to orient towards your values?

Think about it like this: a smooth sea never made a skilled sailor, as a US president once said. Values can be like a lighthouse guiding your way – but that doesn't mean the ocean isn't rough. The more you follow your values, the better you get at it. However, following your values doesn't always feel great or inspiring when you're actually doing it! Sometimes it might include drudgery or even fear. Following your values isn't always a simple linear process either, and it can be hard to stay on course. Here's a story to illustrate what we mean.

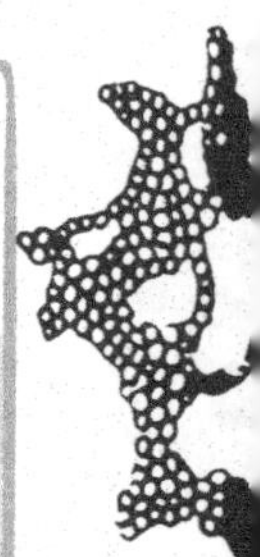

Author spotlight

Hi, Lisa here. When I was a teenager, I used to ride horses.

I was pretty good, and I could ride the ones no one else could ride. But I hadn't ridden in many years until recently, when I started riding a horse called Mac. Here he is.

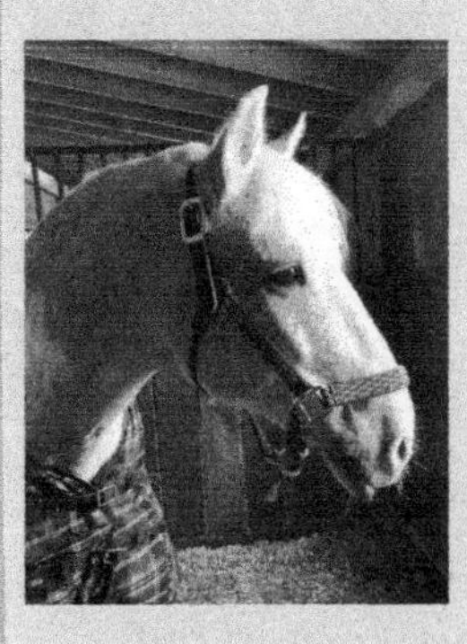

Gorgeous, right? But Mac bucks, and sometimes he sends me flying. So, although I love riding, fear (terror, if I'm truthful) shows up when I go. I have a choice to make – I can opt out, and not keep doing this thing that I love, and which makes me feel alive, or I can go, feeling afraid, and see what happens. To be honest, some days I do opt out – I don't give it my all, we just walk around, and I don't jump him over fences. And on those days, although I feel relieved, that sense of aliveness that I have when I go with my fear dissipates like smoke. Instead, I feel disappointed in myself. Deflated. Regretful.

And there's also this sense of longing, and this thought: "What if I could have…?"

The important thing, though, is continuing to show up, as best I can, staying on this journey to becoming (I hope) a better rider. The only way to do that is, well, riding!

Can you relate to this? Can you think of a time when you moved towards something you cared about, even though it was hard? Maybe you even embodied some of the characteristics of the fictional character you created in the previous chapter? Would you like more of that in your life? Write down one small step that you could take in that direction.

Turning things around, see if you can call to mind a time when you really wanted to do something that aligned with your values, but instead you opted out. See if you can notice what you were feeling before, during, and after the experience of opting out, and the experience of moving towards what you cared about even though it was hard. Write about this below.

Once again, when we start to do things according to our values, our threat-detecting minds try to stop us. They're trying to keep us safe and send us back to the cave. The more we care about something, the bigger the threat.

The good news is that you now have some powerful skills that you've learned from reading this book: curiosity, noticing, opening up your awareness and willingness. Practicing these skills helps you make a mindful choice about pursuing values rather than avoiding anxiety. And then you can actually point your 'values compass' towards the life you want to build, instead of just pointing it away from fear and anxiety.

How to use your values compass

Our 'values compass' helps us orient ourselves towards actions that give us vitality, and aliveness, rather than making life about moving away from our anxiety. Here are the steps to using your compass so that it points you in the direction of what you care about:

1. **Pause.** When you're about to take action, take a moment to connect with your value, whatever one is important.
2. **Notice.** Slow down, expand your awareness, and be curious. Notice the *intention* behind what you are about to do. Are you about to take a step towards what you care about, or are you about to turn away from anxiety or other discomfort?
3. **Choose.** Make a mindful choice to set your compass towards activities that make you feel alive, allowing the anxiety or fear to accompany you on the path.

To use these three steps of 'pause, notice, choose', you'll need to practice the foundational skills we talked about in the previous chapters. So that's noticing, being curious about your experience, opening your awareness to let in all your thoughts and feelings, and having the willingness to allow anxiety to be with you as you step out of your comfort zone and into your discovery zone. Remember, you can choose whether to engage in discovery behavior (take a step towards your value) or to choose comfort behavior (avoid your anxiety).

The fact that we can do things with different intentions is really important, and it reflects an expert level of navigation skill with your values compass. For example, imagine that one of your values is being a good friend. A general choice facing you might be:

- I can be with my friends, and really appreciate and be present with them,

  OR

- I can be with my friends, and totally just be managing my anxiety, and watching in case they think I say something stupid.

When your attention is focused on whether your friends are judging you or not and on self-evaluations, are you really *with* your friends? What things might you not notice if you're stuck in your mind?

Sometimes, when making choices using the three steps, you may see, believe it or not, that joy is actually hanging around there on the fringes of your life along with fear and uncertainty. But if all we ever look for in our lives is the stuff that could possibly go wrong, then that's all we'll notice. All the joyful amazing things are hanging out there too; however, they'll go completely unnoticed because we're so busy shining the light of our attention on all the things we're afraid of.

Now we want to invite you to ask yourself two more questions.

First, how hard is it to have so many of these difficult and scary things on your radar all the time? And second, how willing you are to do something this tough to step towards your values? By this we don't mean how willing you are to have a catastrophe happen; we mean how willing are you to notice the thoughts about catastrophe that show up along the way to acting in a manner that brings you towards the things that are important to you?

Exercise 21: The values compass

In the table opposite, we'd like you to list each of your values on the left and, in the other columns, to write in times you can think of when you've used discovery behaviors to move towards those values, or times when you've used 'comfort behaviors' to stay stuck or move away from them. In the last column, note how alive you felt after you engaged in each behavior.

Please be reassured that we don't judge you for any behaviors that keep you in your comfort zone – we have them too! We just want to notice what brings you towards your values and what doesn't. This is about helping you build your values compass, and finding out what works best for you in navigating your world.

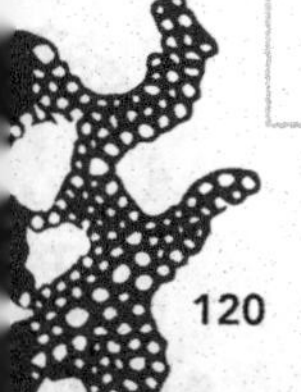

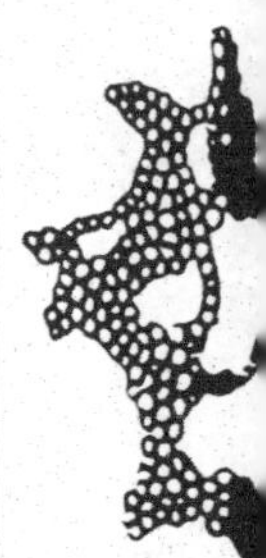

Value	Discovery behaviors	Comfort behaviors	How alive I felt

Test drive

This week, we'd simply like you to keep filling in the values compass table, day by day. Notice when discovery behaviors move you closer to one of your values, and when comfort behaviors move you further away from a value. Remember, discovery behaviors aren't exclusively good and comfort behaviors aren't exclusively bad. All human beings engage in both, and that's fine. We just want you to get curious about which behaviors you tend to use and when you use them, and to notice what works best for you on a given day.

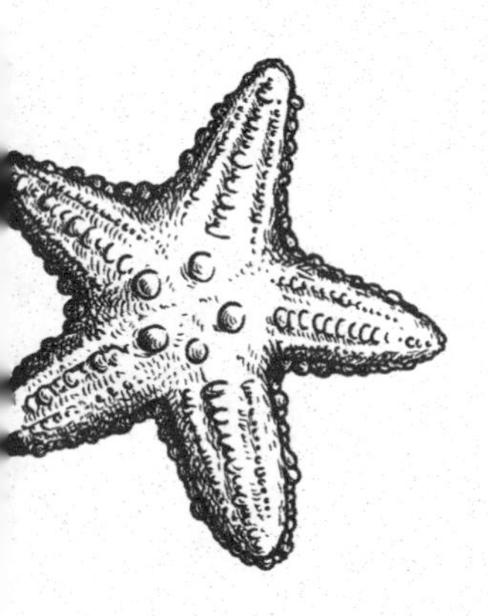

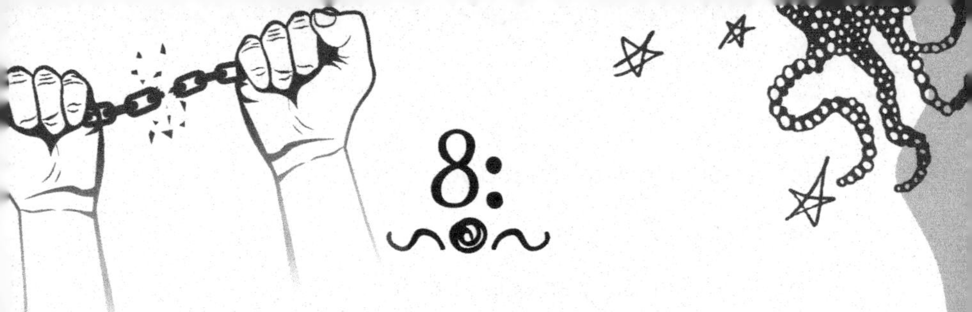

8:

Letting go of the fight with anxiety

In order to begin letting go of your struggle with anxiety, it helps to be curious about the types of things you do to avoid or suppress it – the 'comfort behaviors' we introduced at the end of the last chapter. In other words, what do you do to try to keep yourself in your comfort zone? Usually, most of us have many ways of trying to get rid of anxiety.

Exercise 22: Comfort behaviors

What have *you* done so far to battle your anxiety? Here's a list of common things that people do that might help. Tick off the ones you do.

Pretend it isn't there	
Tell people you're fine	
Ignore people	
Hide what you're thinking	
Not talk about it	
Try to grin and bear it	
Use breathing to distract yourself	

→

Tense your body to defend yourself	
Tell yourself you're fine	
Try not to think any anxious thoughts	
Stay in bed	
Avoid friends	
Not eat	
Try to sleep (but toss and turn)	
Try to think good thoughts not anxious ones	
Argue with your anxiety	
Try to talk yourself out of being anxious	
Try to control your environment	
Avoid certain activities, people and places	
Blame other people for making you anxious	
Blame yourself for feeling anxious	

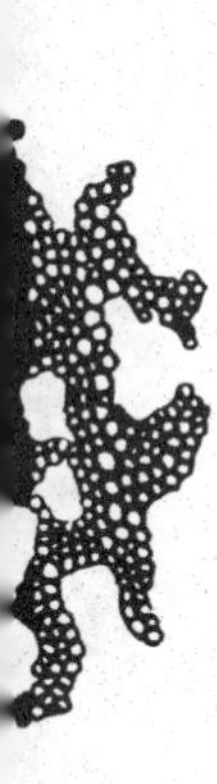

It's quite a list, right? But this is only a tiny sample of the things that people sometimes do in an effort to get away from their anxiety. See if you can think of other things you do and write them in the box below.

Exercise 23: How effective are my comfort behaviors?

Now let's take a moment to see how well all these things work. Use the table below to write in your strategies for managing your anxiety, and then reflect on the effectiveness of each one.

Strategy I use to keep myself safely in my comfort zone	How comfortable I am using this strategy (1 = not at all, 10 = super comfortable)	Does it work? (i.e., does my anxiety go away when I do it?)

Did what you learned in doing this exercise surprise you? If you are like most humans, you probably noticed:

- Your strategies worked, but only a little.
- The more you used a strategy, the more anxious you got.
- Anxiety always seemed to come back, sometimes with a vengeance.
- You felt sad and hopeless because you were trying so hard but not getting very far.

At this point, you might be wondering what's wrong with you – because despite trying all the time to not be anxious, you're still having lots of anxiety.

You might feel like you're just an anxious person. Perhaps you think your mind works differently to the minds of other people you know. There must be *something* wrong with you, right? Because how come nothing works for you the way it seems to work for other people?

Well, we have some news for you: you've fought the good fight. But it isn't you. And there's nothing about you as a person that is making your anxiety stick around.

Let us say that again, in the clearest way we can:

It isn't you that's the problem.

You already have all the tools you need, just as you are.

And one more thing:

It isn't your fault that you're in this struggle.

See if you can let that one sink in for a minute.

It. Is. Not. Your. Fault.

Here's an idea: WHAT IF it isn't you? What if it's the strategy you're using? What if trying to protect yourself from anxiety just… doesn't help… and might even make things worse? Think of it like this. It's kind of like feeding a baby dragon. It nudges you, and you feed it, so it gets quiet for a while. But then it gets hungry again. So it nudges you again, this time a little harder. So you feed it again and maybe you need to feed it a little more this time before it quietens down. Then it gets quiet again. But then, it gets hungry again. And the cycle continues.

Want to know how this story ends? Well, your baby dragon grows up into a giant, formidable fire-breathing beast that could maybe consume you whole. Or char you to a crisp. Yikes!

Hi, Sarah here.

Did you ever have a first impression of someone that was wrong?

I remember having a School Principal who was really strict, and everyone was terribly afraid of her because she had these clickety clack heels that you could hear all the way through the school and she walked really fast. If you heard those heels coming towards your classroom, you knew she meant business and somebody was probably in trouble – people usually sunk down into their desks and hoped she wouldn't look at them!

But I remember later coming to the realisation that a child was being bullied in our school. And that Principal was asking a LOT of questions, and those clickety clack heels never stopped moving from classroom to classroom until the bullying stopped too. Because although the Principal was as tough as nails, she was also fair and she wanted to make sure that every single child in the school was safe and protected.

It took me a while to realize this because I was initially frightened by how this lady came across as so busy and strong and powerful. I didn't realize that kindness came in the same package, because it just wasn't what I was looking for. →

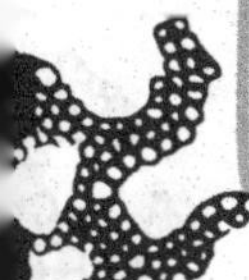

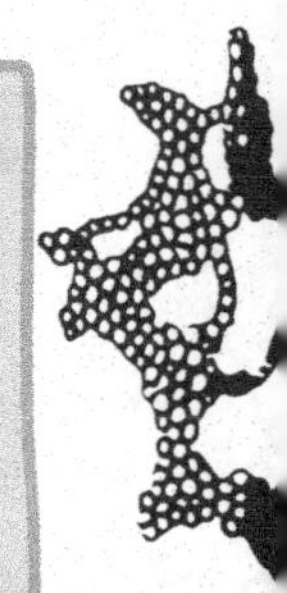

I guess, at the age of five, I also didn't know that you probably had to walk that fast to keep a busy school running smoothly!

So my first impression of her was simply that she was strict – but if I had known how to expand my awareness with curiosity and notice the other details of this person and situation, I might have seen that this Principal was also a protector who was strict so that all of the children in her school were safe. I was too busy avoiding her to realize this!

In Chapter 1, you did several exercises to get to know your anxiety – from drawing it to thinking of it as a fictional character. You might want to refer back to those notes before you complete the next exercise.

Exercise 24: Give it a name

If you were to name your anxiety, what would you call it? It could be something silly, or serious, or childish, or terrifying. Be creative. Think about what name would fit best for you and your anxiety. Maybe your anxiety feels posh, like a 'Winchester'? Or what about something official and important like 'The Committee'? Maybe you'd prefer something silly like 'The Enormous Blob of Stupid Massive Annoyingness' or 'The Hellhole from Hellinghamshire'? Or maybe you'd just give it a nice normal name like 'Sally' or 'Frank'? What feels like a good name to you? Write it below.

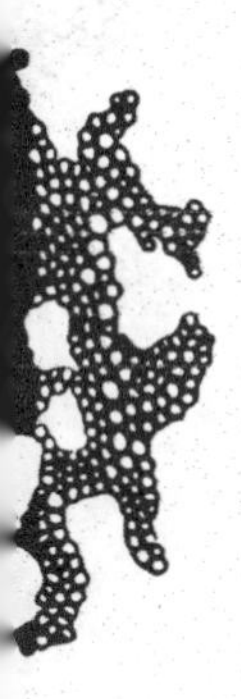

Next, consider when, where and how your anxiety shows up. Like, if you were on a safari and stalking it to get a really good look, where in your life would you find it? List some of these situations or places here.

How did you get on with writing down situations or places where your anxiety tends to show up? We're sure you came up with a few at least. So, now that you have a number of these situations and places written down, take a step back and ask yourself a question: is there anything that links them together? Think about what you learned in Chapter 7 about valuing. For most of us, anxiety is a messenger. It shows up in the middle of things we care deeply about. And, in that sense, it has a lot to tell us about what matters in our lives.

Consider this: think about the little, humdrum, everyday things you do. The boring things that you probably barely remember doing. How often does anxiety hijack those things? We're guessing probably not as often as when you feel the stakes are high, when you're doing something that's really meaningful to you or vital in your life. You see, we're often most afraid when we're at risk of losing or not attaining those things that we care most deeply about.

Given the situations where your anxiety shows up, what do you think that says about what matters to you? Take a few minutes to consider, then write below what you think your anxiety is telling you.

Let's pause and breathe a little bit. We've just thrown a number of ideas at you. Is this a different way of looking at anxiety than you've been used to in the past?

What if anxiety, while unpleasant, isn't something you need to fight or avoid or manage? What if you could treat it like someone who shows up to help you notice what's important to you?

What if, when you start not just to think about it this way, but also to treat it this way, your experience of it changes? What if anxiety doesn't have to be so big that it takes up all of your horizon?

Try this exercise to see what we mean.

Take a moment to get settled in your chair, closing your eyes if that feels comfortable for you. Take a few seconds to just connect with your breath. Breathe in and breathe out again. Do that a few times. And take your time.

As you do that, notice any physical sensations. Notice where anxiety *lives* when it shows up in your body. Just see what parts of your body seem to get activated or tense or wobbly when anxiety shows up. Or maybe it's not tense or wobbly for you. Just whatever happens →

in your body, see if you can really notice *where* in your body anything happens when anxiety shows up.

Some teens find it hard to notice or locate the sensations. If that happens for you, you can just notice that you're not noticing any part of your body feeling a body sensation. That's a good observation too.

Notice also any emotions that arise for you. Observe as they come and go, shift and change. Notice thoughts, and how they come and go. Maybe you might tense up. If that happens, practice unclenching your body and noticing instead the emotions that come with those thoughts.

Do this for a few minutes, breathing in and out. Staying connected to your breath. Your mind might tend to wander to other places, and that's okay. That's just what minds do. Any time you notice your mind wandering, just gently bring it back to your breath again.

When you are ready, take a few deep breaths and a stretch, and allow yourself to open your eyes.

Here's the thing: if you head towards your values by doing the things that are important to you, then it's highly likely that anxiety will come along for the ride. You don't have to like it, love it or want it. But the more you try to fight, manage or avoid it – or treat it like it is absolutely unacceptable – and the more you treat yourself as unable to move unless it goes away, the bigger it gets and the more stuck you get.

So, what about experimenting with allowing it to be like a traveling companion? What if we told you that it can walk with you when you're going places? What if we said that it can talk to you, but there's no need to let it block your path or make you choose which way to go? You can listen to it if you want, of course, but you still get to decide whether or not to do what it says. In other words, even if it is there with you, you get to choose your own direction! You're in charge, not your anxiety.

Test drive

Over the next week, practice thinking about your anxiety using the name you gave it in Exercise 24. Use your skills of noticing, being curious, and expanding your awareness to see what happens to your anxiety when you try to avoid it, when you listen to it, when you don't listen to it, and when you simply let it accompany you on your journey. Record your experiences below.

9: Understanding the thinky part of anxiety

One part of anxiety that can be really hard is the thinky part. Or, if you prefer, the talky part. And anxiety talks. A LOT. As we've said in other chapters, it's kind of like a backseat driver who insists on going along on every adventure that matters to you, AND NEVER SHUTS UP, EVER.

What's worse? Your anxiety knows you. It has studied you, and it knows how best to scare you – ESPECIALLY when you're trying something that really matters to you.

Have you ever had a day, week, month or hour where worry and anxiety would relentlessly annoy you? During those times, was it like a large, overbearing, over-affectionate dog that just insisted on bothering you? Sitting on you while you're minding your own business on the couch? Slobbering in your food? Standing in front of the TV so you can't see it? Maybe you kept pushing it out of the way or trying to move around it or telling it to go away, but nothing worked?

Us too.

So – what do you do when your anxiety never shuts up and ONLY talks about stuff that scares you? I mean, are you supposed to just let it be? That's hard! And you might notice your body becoming really anxious and tense and stressed, because nothing you do works.

This is a GREAT place to practice noticing, being curious, opening up your awareness and cranking up your willingness dial to see how it all works.

What do you usually do when this happens? Try to ignore it? Tell yourself you didn't want to watch TV anyway? Try to talk yourself out of being so worried? Us too! That's normal, isn't it? When you don't like something, you try to get rid of it. Like if a big dog was annoying you, you might try to push it off the couch.

Here's the thing about over-affectionate dogs though: the more you push them away, the harder they try to snuggle with you. And it works the same way with anxiety. The more you push it away, the closer it gets.

So now what?

Well, see if you can pretend your anxiety is a new toy you can play with – a bit like you did with your mind in Chapter 2. Let's see how it actually works, instead of how it says it works!

Exercise 25: Chocolicious...

Let's play a game. It's really simple – all you need to do is think of your favorite chocolate bar. See if you can picture it in your mind. Maybe imagine holding it in your hand or unwrapping it. See if you can smell it. Mmmmm.

Now – and here's the fun part – imagine what it tastes like if you take a bite. Yummmm! The silky texture of the chocolate melting on your tongue, and the creamy sweetness of it. Take your time to imagine and savor every part of the experience.

What did you notice about the experience of doing this exercise? Did your mouth start to water a bit? Are you hungry? Did you put this book down and go to get an actual chocolate bar? Or did you want to?

If you did any of those things, you've just experienced what we call 'fusion'. What we mean by fusion is just our bodies' tendency to react to thoughts as though they are real, literal truths. There's no actual chocolate bar here (unless you went to get yourself one). But perhaps your mouth watered, or you felt a pang of hunger. All from just thinking about that chocolate bar!

So, when an anxious thought arises in your mind, your body reacts the same way – as though the thought is real. Next time you notice a worry thought, slow yourself down and notice how your body feels. Notice what your body is doing, and take a moment or two to write it below:

Now, it's time for chocolate again! Remember that delicious chocolate bar you imagined eating? Well, now we want you to STOP THINKING ABOUT IT! Right now! Don't stop until there is absolutely no trace of that chocolate bar left in your mind. Go!

Do your best here...

How's it going? Is it gone yet?

How can you tell?

Are you thinking about something else? What's that?

And how do you know it's the right thing to think about? Just because it's not a choc... OOPS!

Uh-oh. There it is. That pesky chocolate bar again.

You've just discovered a little problem. In order not to think about something, you have to keep it in your mind so you can tell if you're not thinking about it.

Get it? Every time you check to see if you're not thinking about that thing… you think about the thing!

And anxiety? Turns out, there's no way to run away from anxious thoughts in your head. It just doesn't work the way running away from bees works. There's no running or hiding. There's no talking yourself out of them. There's no pushing them down off the couch.

This is a pretty rotten state of affairs, isn't it?

So, now what?

Well, the first thing to know is that… anxious thoughts aren't big dogs. I mean, you can think about dogs. You could imagine a big dog right now. But can that big dog in your mind bite you? Right here, right now?

Nope. It's just a thought. Well, it's a thought-dog.

And what about your chocolate bar? Can you actually take a bite of it now? Or share it with us (pleeaasse!)? But nope. It's just a chocolate thought-bar.

So, if you can't eat thought-chocolate, and thought-dogs can't slobber on you, what does this mean?

Maybe, just maybe, there's no need to run away from your anxious thoughts. Because firstly, as you've

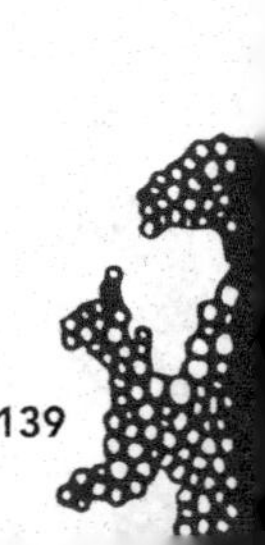

discovered, it doesn't work very well. And secondly, thoughts are just that. They're thoughts. They might be scary or uncomfortable. They might come with horrible feelings in your body. And you might not like them or want them. Or you might wish they wouldn't hang around so much. Or surprise you when they pop in.

But guess what? We don't get to choose the thoughts in our head. We know. That's really annoying. But also it's the truth. Remember trying not to think about the chocolate? Yup. We didn't get very far with that.

We aren't in control of our thoughts any more than we're in control of the weather. Rainstorms just blow in sometimes. And then the sun comes out. It just happens. The same way the thoughts in our head just happen.

But here's the good news! There *is* something you can do when your head is full of anxious, worried thoughts. Something that works better than trying to run from them, push them down, argue with them or fight with them. And the best way to learn it is to try it out!

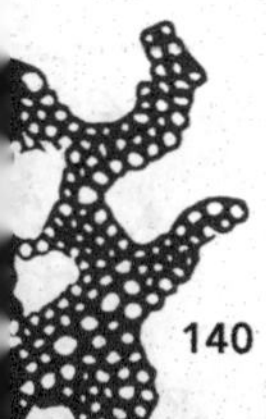

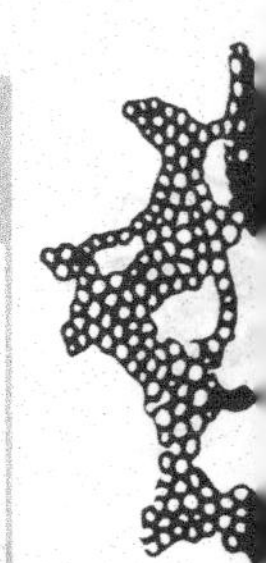

Exercise 26: Stepping back and noticing my thoughts

This exercise is about slowing your thoughts down so you can notice what they are. Take a few nice deep breaths, sit back, and take a peek at what your anxious thoughts are. Take five minutes and see how many you can write below.

When you're done, see if you can notice your own feelings and the sensations in your body. What was it like *not* to run away from your anxious thoughts, but instead to notice and label them? Look at them right there on the page. Look at the lines that make up the letters in each word. Look at the spaces between the words. Notice what color the words are in. See how many letters make up one of your thoughts.

Now, take a moment, and think back to when you began this book. Compare how you felt about your anxious thoughts then – when you were running away from them – to now, when you've spent some time playing with them, noticing them, and being curious about them. What did you discover? Did some of them lose their sting? Maybe just a little bit?

You're starting to learn some different things that you can do when your head is humming with anxious thoughts.

You can:

- label them
- notice them
- write them down
- draw them
- talk about them
- play with them
- give them silly names
- sing about them

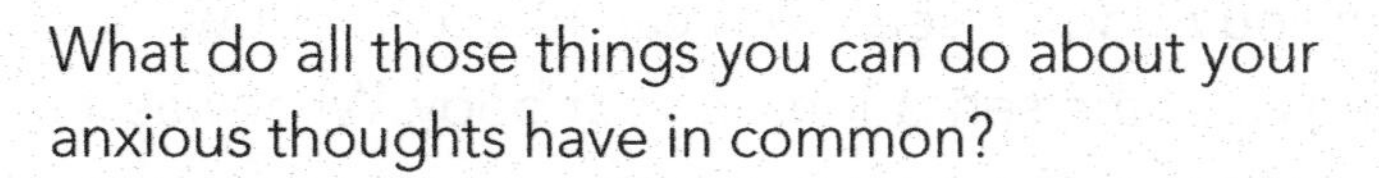

What do all those things you can do about your anxious thoughts have in common?

The answer is that none of them involve running away! Instead, All those things involve *stepping back and observing them without reacting to or fighting them.*

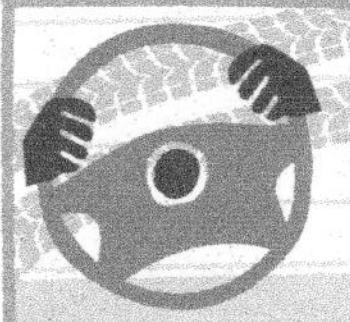

Test drive

This week, just practice noticing your thoughts, and letting them come and go. You can do this by trying out some of the following:

- slowing down
- noticing what they are
- labeling them as thoughts
- letting them come and go as they please

This new skill will take some time to master. Sometimes it helps to practice with non-anxious thoughts and to label them out loud, before you move on to try the same thing with the thoughts that worry you. Keep trying; you can even practice with other people too! Be curious about how it will work as you go through your day.

10: Taming the thinky part of anxiety – defusion

When you struggle with anxiety, it can feel like your mind is streaming a 'doom and gloom' YouTube channel all the time, 24/7. Why is it like that? Let's think back to our threat detector, shall we?

You see, it can get pretty exhausting if we try to push the dog off the couch each time we have an anxious thought. We have forty to seventy thousand thoughts a day, so that could be a lot of pushing! And it can be overwhelming to feel all the emotions elicited by these thoughts. They might even change your idea of who you are. Like, it might feel like YOU ARE YOUR ANXIETY! Rather than anxiety is your backseat driver.

But let's slow down and get curious again, practicing some of the strategies you learned in the previous chapters. Thoughts only matter if as we treat them like they are the real thing. They only have power over us if we actually believe that they are true. But here's the thing – remember that as threat detectors, our minds are overly focused on threat, and they are overinclusive of threat. This means that our minds are naturally wired – evolved, really – to think waaaay more things are threats than are actually real and true threats.

Take, for example, our minds' tendency to spend time in the future, making predictions of terrible things that might happen, or horrible embarrassments that might befall us, or other types of fears and doubts and scary images. Let's say you have a school social event to go to and you're not a terribly social kind of a person. And your mind tells you that if you go to this thing....

No one who is going to want to hang out with you. And everyone will notice you walking around alone, and it will be terrible. You will be ruined. Everyone will know you have no friends and that no one wants to be your friend. No one wants to be your friend because you are just a loser, and everyone knows it too.

Jeez, we have to stop there because suddenly we're back in school hearing to our sixteen-year-old minds saying exactly the same thing to us. Seriously. Ouch!

Eeeucchhhh. If reading those words resonated with you, slow down and see what emotions you're feeling, how they're reverberating in your body, and what they push you to want to do. You see, it's this last part, this tendency for us to feel the bite of those thoughts and then try to fix the situation, that hooks us. We might fall back to trying to push our anxiety away, for example. And the very moment we do that, we're trapped by it. It's all we see, our whole horizon.

But what if there's something different we could do?

You see, even though anxiety is a backseat driver that talks to us all the time, we don't need to believe everything it says. It likes to avoid risks, and if it had its way it would stop you going on any adventures at all! The trick is to practice allowing it to talk to you, making space for the feelings that arise when it does, and then keeping your distance. Here's what we mean.

Let's imagine that your backseat driver is yapping away at you one fine summer's evening. Maybe you call your anxiety Frank, and Frank is telling you what a big baby you are and that you can't ever get anything right and you have no friends and you'll only make a fool of yourself if you go anywhere so just stay the hell home!

So, if you're experiencing those kinds of thoughts, you might feel pushed to do a number of things. Maybe you'll go to the school social and not talk to anyone; or if you do talk to someone, you might second guess whether they really like you, or are just being nice, or will make fun of you later behind your back. Or you might decide not to go at all. But here's the problem if you made that last choice… you'd never learn whether those thoughts were helpful or unhelpful.

However, if you were a person who was able to slow down, step back, and notice your thoughts as simply information that may or may not be helpful, you might make different choices based on what was important to you. For example, you might go and try saying hello to people you were interested in hanging out with and sticking around to see how that actually worked.

But we're getting ahead of ourselves here, aren't we?! How does one 'step back' from one's thoughts? Let's do an exercise, if you're willing.

Exercise 27: Writing with your wrong hand

In the space below, try writing your thoughts down using your non-dominant hand. That means you should write with the hand you don't usually write with. Do this, slowly, noticing what it's like to write with the wrong hand, watching each letter unfold, noticing the scrape of the pen on the paper. Notice them, letter by letter, watching the shapes spill across the page. Remember to breathe as you do this.

What was that like, observing your thoughts outside of your body? Read through them slowly, speaking each word to yourself, in your mind. Do this perhaps five to ten times. Stay curious, and see what you notice about this experience. See if you can hold any expectations you have about this exercise lightly.

When you did this exercise, what did you notice about your experience of having these thoughts? Perhaps you noticed that they have less bite, or are less evocative of emotion? Perhaps you're starting to notice that you can experience them for what they are – 'mental weather' that changes constantly and naturally – and that you don't have to manage them or do anything with them at all, other than let them come and go as they please.

Perhaps you're starting to notice that if you accept the fact that you don't have to believe your thoughts, they have no power over you.

Here's one more simple exercise you can practice in the real world as you go through your day. You can do it whether you're anxious or not, whenever you think of it – just to build your skill in stepping back and noticing thoughts as part – and not all – of your experience.

Exercise 28: Making space

Think of an anxious thought that bothers you a lot – one that seems to keep popping up in your experience. See if you can choose one that is a bit triggering, perhaps a negative self-evaluation. Examples might be, "I'm a loser", "I'm a failure" or "I'm not good enough." Write your thought in the space below, slowly, letting it sink in as though it is true:

Now write the same thing down again, slowly, but this time so it follows the stem "I'm having the thought that":

I'm having the thought that

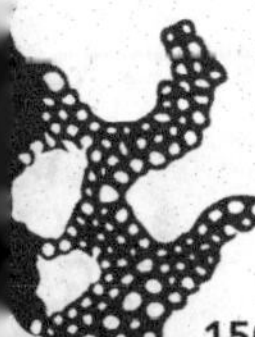

Now do it again, but this time so it follows the stem "I'm noticing that I'm having the thought that":

I'm noticing that I'm having the thought that

Now do it again, but this time so it follows the stem "I'm aware of noticing that I'm having the thought that":

I'm aware of noticing that I'm having the thought that

Take a few moments to reflect on your experience. Did you notice anything different about having these types of thoughts? Did you notice that there was a little more space between you and them? And maybe, just maybe, did the emotions they evoked feel a bit different? Do you have a different perspective on them, just a little bit?

Here's the thing: if you did the exercises above, you just spent a huge amount of time with your anxious thoughts – on purpose. You brought them into your awareness, you thought about them, you wrote them down and you read them back to yourself. Basically, you spent some quality time with them – which is the exact opposite of avoiding them. In fact, it's kind of like what you'd do with a friend. Isn't that interesting? You let those anxious thoughts in on purpose. And in doing that, you reduced their power over you.

Totally counterintuitive, we know. But anxiety?

Well, it doesn't always tell the truth.

Test drive

This week, try to notice any time your mind feels anxious and tries to do something with that anxiety. If, in a given situation and moment, your mind generates a lot of thoughts about what is happening and you find yourself getting fused with your thoughts, practice stepping back from them by adding "I'm noticing that I'm having the thought that" or "I'm aware of noticing that I'm having the thought that". See how it goes – we're curious to hear what you find out!

11:

The you beyond your anxiety

If anxiety wrote a story about you, what would it say?

Imagine if you could describe yourself from the perspective of your anxiety, as though anxiety were another person who thought they knew you. Imagine anxiety knew what you could handle, and what you couldn't. Imagine it knew what you were capable of, and what would level you. Pretend to be the voice of your own anxiety and describe yourself below.

What is it like looking at yourself from this perspective? Is there a part of you that sees yourself this way too, and agrees with it? But more importantly, is there another part of you that doesn't? That wonders if, maybe, more is possible? Take a few moments to connect with that voice. Your anxiety won't like it. In fact, we suspect that this activity will engage your threat detector so that it gets pretty loud. Still, who likes being told what to do? Go ahead, slow down, and get quiet, and have a listen to that other, quieter voice.

What does it wish for? What does it miss most, that your struggle with anxiety has taken? What does it wonder about? What does it want to do? Take a little time and listen as closely and honestly as you can. See if you can give this voice a microphone to amplify it for a while. Is it telling another story of you, a different story than the one you're used to? In a world where it was possible to be the best version of you, what would that version of you be like? See if you can slow down, get quiet, and listen deeply to that voice. Then take a deep breath, and write the new story of you here.

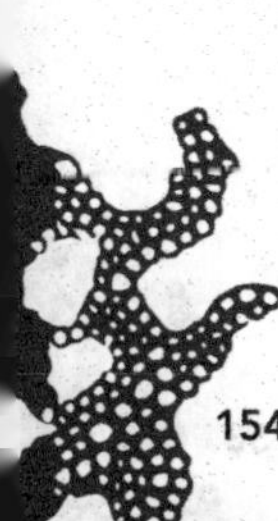

Just like you learned in Chapter 10 how to step back from thoughts, you can also learn to step back from the stories of you that your anxiety spins. What if that's all they are – stories, and stories that you can hold lightly?

Here's an idea: in each moment, a new story of you can emerge with just one different decision. Just one, in one single moment. All you have to do is make a single decision or take a single step that is different from what you've done before. Anxiety can be very loud, and when it shouts its stories about what's possible for you, it can be hard not to believe them and not to try to live within the bounds of those stories. But the first move in stepping out of anxiety's story of you is to practice noticing it for what it is – simply a story.

Let's try something. Pick up your phone and find the most recent selfie you took. Don't cheat, just look at the last one. Does it sum you up completely? Does it capture the essence of who you are – all the memories, the brilliance and silliness, the sense of humour, the kindness, all the aspects of you?

No? We didn't think so. It wouldn't be possible for a single snapshot of you in any one moment to sum you up in entirety. That's a silly thought even to consider, isn't it? And yet, when anxiety shows up and tells us a story of what's possible for us – of what we can and can't do – we buy into it hook, line, and sinker. It's amazing how compelling anxiety can be, isn't it?

You see, there are lots of different versions of you at different times in your life. Try out the next exercise to explore this idea in more detail.

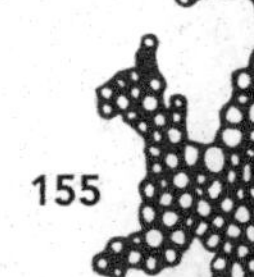

Exercise 29: Different versions of me

Think about a younger version of you. It helps to bring to mind you at a specific age, in a particular situation. Imagine this in as much detail as you can. What was that version of you like way back then? Write your thoughts below.

Now, go back to the best possible version of you that you imagined earlier in this chapter. What qualities do they bring to bear? How do they act in the world? What would they want to be about? Tell us about the best version of you.

→

Take a few moments to think about one of your worst moments – maybe one in which you were struggling, or feeling vulnerable, or not at all proud of yourself. Tell us about this version of you in your worst moment.

Now, take a few moments to imagine an older version of you – say five or ten years older. This version of you has come through many hardships and has hacked their anxiety. They are thriving. Describe this version of you.

Here's a cool thing that you've just been practicing if you completed the exercise above: there's one you – a 'noticing' you – that is observing all these stories about who you are. That observing self, while it notices these stories, is separate from them. And it has been there since the day you were born – since you took your very first breath. It is the same regardless of whether you're young or older, or in your best or worst moments. You can think of your observing self as stepping into a perspective where you can notice these stories of who you are, and recognise that they're just that – stories. Once you step into this perspective, you're free.

What we mean is this: we are much, much more than the stories our mind spins about us. We could never be summed up by our best or worst moments, or by our young or older selves. And that means we're much, much more than the story that anxiety spins about us. The best part is, once you step into your observing self, you have the freedom to choose your next steps, and whether they'll be in line with anxiety's story – or in line with your values. In your observing self perspective, you can choose to be flexible, and to orientate yourself in whatever direction your heart longs to go.

Test drive

This week, do some imagining. Pretend there is a different version of you – someone you really like and admire. You believe they know what to do, and they're strong, and you trust them. Perhaps they're older, and they know how to manage anxiety. Perhaps they're like a good, honest friend who can and will call you out on all your nonsense. Either way, they really see and really know you. They know the very deepest parts of you, even the parts that have been buried, and whose voices have been choked off by anxiety. There is a you that trusts you and believes in you. A wiser, kinder version of you. Imagine them as you go through your week, and keep in mind the words of the poet Padraig O'Tuama:

There is a you
Telling another story of you.
Listen to her.

12:

Breaking free of the anxiety cage

If you've made it through the last few chapters and you're practicing the principles in them, then you may have got to a place where you're no longer letting anxiety push you around much. You may be beginning to taste a little freedom and flexibility, and the world might be starting to feel just a little bit more roomy.

Pretty cool, huh? But wait, there's more for you to learn, to make the world feel even roomier! If you're just getting started on taming that backseat driver of yours, then you're setting some limits with your anxiety. Perhaps you aren't allowing anxiety to drive anymore, or to run you off the road at least. Cool! But what might it look like to really go after it?

Here's what we know: setting some limits around what your anxiety tells you to do can get you a long way down the road. It can be so helpful, and right now you might just be seeing the light at the end of the tunnel. But really turning towards anxiety and deliberately trying to trigger it, to invite it in, to get it loud so you can teach it that no matter how big it gets you won't do what it says? That's the secret to lasting freedom and flexibility.

Exercise 30: Facing your fears

So, if you decide to really go after your anxiety, what might that look like? Here are some ideas for you! We call them 'exposures'.

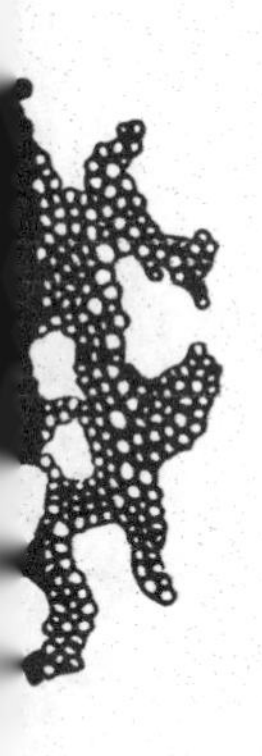

- If you're anxious about walking up to a group of other teens, walk straight in and say hello! Listen in and find a spot to join the conversation.
- If you're worried about trying a new food, make a habit of doing just that! Make it a thing you do at home as well as when out with friends.
- If you're afraid to experience a new thing because you're worried that you might fail at it or look stupid, do it anyway – and seek out new things to try, just to push back against your anxiety!
- If you feel weird touching a surface that might be contaminated or dirty, just plop your hand on it. Then rub it with your fingers or even your face!

When you initially try out these things, your anxiety will try to fight back. First, it will escalate, get all up in your face and get super loud – it will hate that you're doing these things! Your body might be in revolt – ready to run, heart pounding, dizzy, sweaty palms, butterflies in your stomach. But if you stay, your anxiety will learn that it can't push you around – that you won't bow down to it anymore, and that you'll keep winning these battles.

When you choose to engage in battles and deliberately seek exposure to the things that make you anxious, always keep your 'why' in mind. Why are you doing this?

Remember your values from Chapters 6 and 7? Write them here to help you keep them front and centre in your mind.

My value(s):

Now take a little time to consider some ways (or at least one, to start) in which you can really *go after* your anxiety. Write them down in the space below.

Ways of going after my anxiety:

If you go after your anxiety in the ways you've identified above, in order to live consistently with the values you've chosen for yourself, then you'll set yourself on a path towards freedom – towards that light at the end of the tunnel. You see, going after

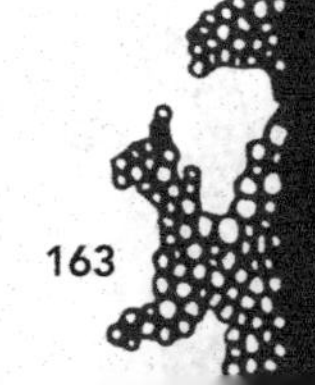

anxiety isn't primarily about vanquishing it – it's about carving out a bigger space in your life for you to be the person you most want to be, and to do the things you most care about doing. If you feel ready to make a commitment to going for this, try the next exercise.

Exercise 31: Committing to action

Finish the sentence below, and slow down and notice what it feels like to write it all out.

If (write your way of going after your anxiety here)

____

____

is a huge step towards (write your value here)

____

____

then I am willing to go for it and feel whatever might show up, even if it is (write down any thoughts and feelings you might have during your exposure)

____

____

Deep breath! How did that feel? See if you can notice all the thoughts and feelings that are showing up inside you right now. Notice also if there is a feeling of aliveness and vitality that comes along with fear, anxiety and whatever discomfort may also be there. You've got this!

In taking such bold steps to really go after anxiety, it's important to understand that you don't need to do this alone. It's okay to ask your parents or friends to support you to do these really hard things. You can build a team! A squad! A posse! A platoon to support you as you go on the attack. And even though it can be hard to ask for help, it's so important if you really want to go after your anxiety.

Exercise 32: Building a team

If you could build a dream team of people to help you face your fears, to support you as you go, who would you choose, and why? Write your thoughts below.

Now we're going to invite you to make a committed action – something that moves you towards your values, and that will help you in facing your fears. If you're willing, think about a promise you can make to yourself – one you'll keep, no matter what – that will help you to be courageous. We suggest either writing down an 'exposure' or fear-facing action, or choosing someone to be on your support team who will cheer you on as you go. Or both!

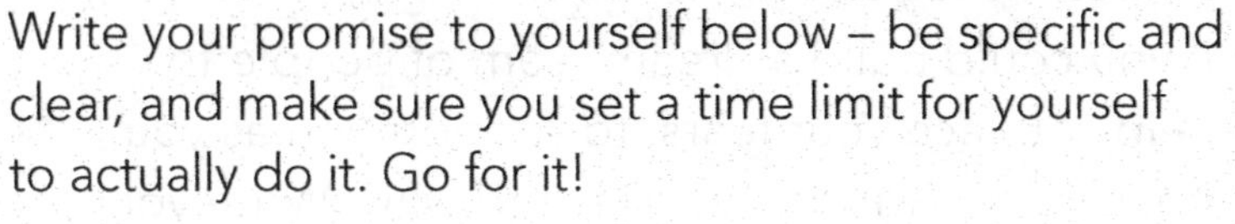

Write your promise to yourself below – be specific and clear, and make sure you set a time limit for yourself to actually do it. Go for it!

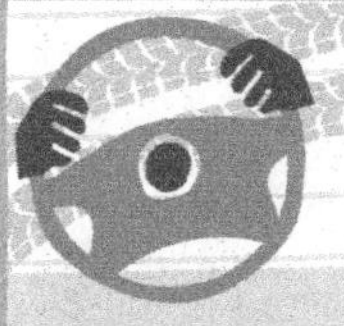

Test drive

This week, do as many exposures as you can and write down below what you observed happening as you did them. Did you get closer to your values? It's okay if you did get closer, and it's okay if you didn't. Just notice what happens. We're exploring and learning. We're pioneers, out to discover what's possible for us, what makes us feel whole and alive. So take your time and savor these experiences. See you in the next chapter!

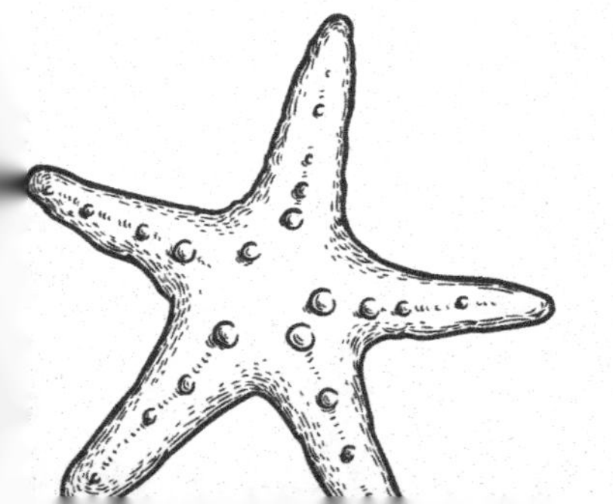

13: Saying yes and meaning it

We began this book by talking about anxiety, and how it can feel like it is putting you in a cage. We talked about how it can shrink your perspective, making it so small that it becomes just your anxiety and you. We discussed how it can inhabit you so fully that it becomes hard to tell the difference between you and it – where you end and it begins.

But, as we hope you've now discovered, you're so much more than your anxiety. In fact, its only power over you comes from what you allow it to have. It turns out that if you let your anxiety get up close, and be as loud and uncomfortable as it wants, and then you don't believe it and don't do what it says, it actually has no hold over you at all.

Over time, this practice of staying and facing your anxiety, of remaining willing to experience discomfort, will teach it to give up and go away. And meanwhile, each step you take into your anxiety is another step over a threshold to a life that is new, roomier, more vital and more free.

By stepping back from your mind and taking time to think about what is important to you, you get to choose how you build your life. And yes, of course, many difficult and tricky things will happen along the way, but you've already got everything you need to live the life you want to live.

So – it's time to start building, and lots of things we want to build are first developed in our imagination and then put into action. Each and every moment is an opportunity to change the course of your life, by making just one different decision or one bold and novel action that you haven't done or tried before. And each bold action is like a stone in the foundation of a different and vibrant life that you can continue to build one small act at a time.

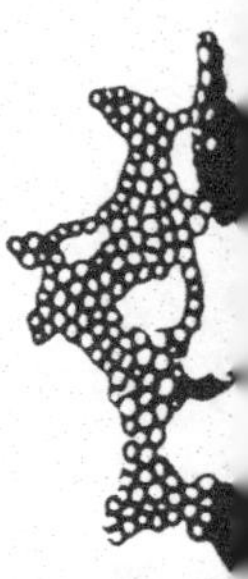

Exercise 33: Visualizing my best life

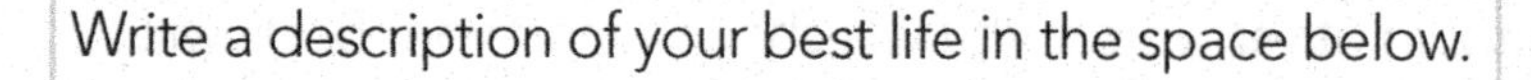

It's time to dream big now. What kind of life can you imagine for yourself? Let your mind and heart go, and imagine that anything might be possible, no matter what your mind tells you to the contrary. Let it soar!

Write a description of your best life in the space below.

And how do you start to build this new life? As Brené Brown says, "You get to courage by couraging". Now, if you want to run a marathon and you spend most of your time on your couch, it won't be possible for you to run all that distance tomorrow. But in six months, with the right gradual, systematic training? You could, if you wanted to. In other words, you will change, and your body will change, through what you *do* rather than what you *think* about doing. And similarly, you can retrain your anxious brain by *doing* something rather than *thinking* about it.

Consider what your actions might need to look like in order for you to build your new and better life. What small, gradual, systematic practices can you engage in? What tiny, bold, courageous acts? For example, if you want to do something brave, like travel alone when you've always travelled with your parents or friends, you might want to work your way up to that by practicing. What other actions might you need to take to get the life you'd like in the future, or even the one you'd like next week?

Exercise 34: Bold steps and actions

Write below some examples of bold steps you might make in your life that will help you become the person you most want to be.

Now, we know that this isn't always going to be easy, but we believe you've got what it takes to have the life you want. In fact, we think you always had it, but we're really pleased that you brought us along on your journey.

Let's do one last mindfulness piece. Like we said, we think you've already got all you need to build a life that's bold, spacious, and worthy of you. Furthermore, we know that everyone has fears, and most people will have to face them along the way. And interestingly, the more willing you are to open yourself up to this difficult and scary stuff, and to look at it with curiosity, the easier it is.

Counterintuitive!

Close your eyes and imagine yourself feeling free.

Imagine that your anxiety is still there – because after all, it's part of you too (and you might need it someday when your friend tells you to jump off a high dive and you can't swim…) – but imagine that you've discovered that you don't actually need to get rid of it after all.

What would it mean to be free?

What would that look like?

What sorts of things might you need to do to get there?

Yes, we know it might sometimes be hard, but let's really imagine you knowing what you need to do and doing it, again and again and again.

You've braved this storm, and you'll brave many more.

Breathe that in, to all the versions of you. Step into the observing you. You've got this. We believe in you. Breathe in and breathe out. Notice your chest rising and falling. Notice the places in your body that touch the chair. Notice the chair that holds you. Notice that the floor beneath you supports you and the chair.

Notice that you've done this, all of this, and you can do it again as many times as you need to. →

We believe in you.

And what would it be like, if from this moment forth, you believed in you too? Say to yourself some small phrase that you might wish a coach, a loving friend, a parent or a grandparent would say to you in a difficult moment, and hear those words again and again. Let them wash over you. Breathe them into all the parts of you.

You've got this. Every time. Every single time.

Now open your eyes and have a fresh look at this marvelous world that is just waiting for you.

Test drive

Over the next week, we want you to write your top tips for reminding yourself anytime you might forget that you've already got what it takes. What might 'Next Week You' need to remember to do small bold acts? What might 'Next Month You' need to remember when Frank (or whatever you call your anxiety) gets too loud and forgets that he's supposed to be helping you and not preventing you from doing all the stuff you love?

14:

Nobody's perfect – practicing self-kindness

Congratulations on making it through the book!

We hope that you've tried out some of the ideas and techniques that we've presented. Remember that these are practices – and practices are things that, over time, you can strengthen. You're not supposed to be good at them right from the start! This is new. And if you've struggled with anxiety for a long time, it can be really hard to give up the strategies you used in the past – even if deep down you know that they aren't really helping you much.

It's okay. We get it. Please give yourself a big pat on the back for doing the hard work simply to get yourself started. We think you're a rock star! Seriously.

You might be worried that you didn't learn all the stuff perfectly, or that you didn't practice it enough, or that you had some hard days, weeks or even months when you gave in to your anxiety. We know. And that's a normal part of learning how to face your fears. Nobody's perfect, and nobody gets it right all the time. We're all works in progress – even your parents (and even us, even though we wrote a whole book on how to cope with anxiety!).

It's okay. This can be really hard. We know.

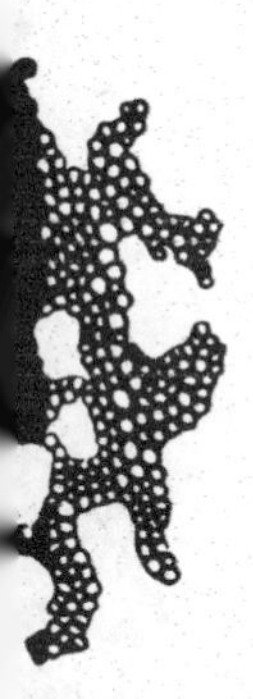

Have you ever noticed how harshly you can speak to yourself when you don't feel like you did stuff properly or well enough? If so, you're not alone. Our minds work like that too. In fact, everyone's minds work like that. We can all be pretty hard on ourselves sometimes. And, because our minds are our threat detectors, and because they've evolved to protect us – which is a seriously important job – sometimes they can be harder on us than anyone else. By rushing to pick out all our flaws before anyone else does, perhaps they'll be able to keep us safe – right?

And you'll remember from Chapter 2 that our minds are way overinclusive of danger. This tendency to be over the top also bleeds into our minds' tendency to be self-critical. Sometimes part of the threat detection work your mind does is making sure you feel bad about stuff you didn't do well. It does this so that, if it can make you feel bad enough, maybe you'll work harder and do better next time.

Have you ever noticed, when you felt like you didn't do a good job, or that you disappointed others, or that you failed at something, having thoughts like:

- I'm just not good enough
- I'll never get it right
- There's something wrong with me
- I just can't do it
- It's just too hard
- Everyone will be disappointed
- I'm so bad at this
- What's the point, anyway?

Sometimes you might even feel as though you need your internal critic to be so mean – or else you might make mistakes, or not be able to do all the things you're trying to do. But is that really the case?

Often, this kind of self-talk just kind of makes us feel sad and bad. What about you? You see, even though your mind is a threat detector, it's not always helpful in how it tries to keep us safe. Sometimes – like when it goes all negative on us – it isn't helpful at all. And we're not saying that your mind has to be positive all the time. It doesn't. Some days just have bad things in them, and it would be unusual if we didn't notice that or pretended that it made us happy. The most important thing to remember here is that you aren't alone if you feel this way.

So, what do you do when this happens – when your mind talks to you in negative, self-critical ways? Well, you can cultivate a different sort of voice to talk to yourself.

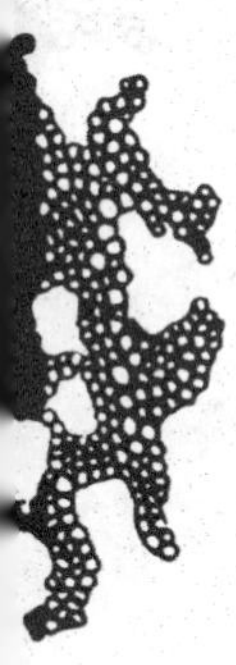

Exercise 35: The wise and kind guide

Imagine you have a guide, a coach or a teacher inside of you – someone who is always wise and kind. This person knows you well – they've seen every moment of your life, and they know all your secrets. They've seen you at your best, and at your worst. And they have some wisdom to share with you.

Take a few moments to write a letter to yourself from this wise, kind guide. Stay curious and open to what they have to say.

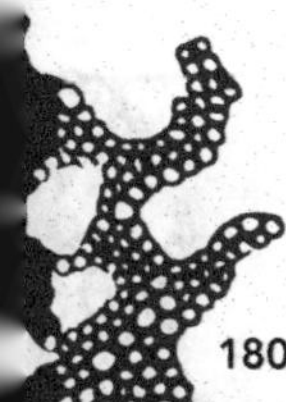

Let the experience of having done this exercise wash over you. See if you can let in whatever the guide shared with you. It can be hard to let in kindness, to give yourself permission to not beat yourself up for falling short – for being human. We've been there too. Slow down, and remember that taking care of yourself is a key part of building a life you love.

The skill you're learning here is called 'self-kindness'. It just means being kind to yourself – and while that sounds really obvious, it takes practice to get into the habit of it.

Sometimes it's harder to be kind to yourself than to others, so you can practice saying kind things to people in your family – to your parents, siblings, aunties and uncles, grandparents or cousins, for example. Try that out and see how it works. And don't forget to try it on yourself too!

You might notice that speaking to yourself kindly is more helpful than speaking to yourself in a critical way. After all, if you could choose a boss to work for, would you choose one who picked apart everything you did, or one who was steady and encouraging, making space for you to make mistakes as a necessary part of learning?

To help deepen this skill, consider how that wise guide or supportive boss might talk with you if you made a mistake, or if you didn't do as well as you hoped or expected at something. Below are some examples to get you started, and to help you along your journey.

- "Falling down is a necessary part of learning to fly."
- "It's okay to make mistakes."
- "You've got this."
- "Next time you'll do it better."
- "Well done for trying!"
- "It's okay to try again tomorrow!"
- "Nobody's perfect!"
- "You're doing the best you can!"
- "Be gentle with yourself!"
- "Everybody has hard days!"
- "It's okay to ask for help!"
- "I believe in you. I really, really do."

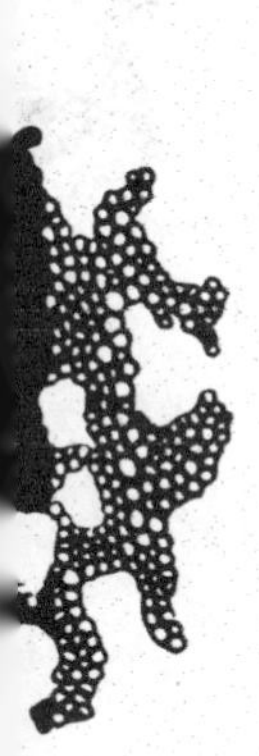

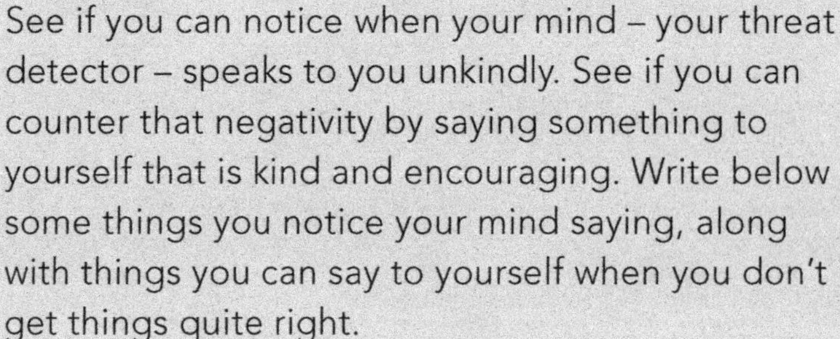

Test drive

See if you can notice when your mind – your threat detector – speaks to you unkindly. See if you can counter that negativity by saying something to yourself that is kind and encouraging. Write below some things you notice your mind saying, along with things you can say to yourself when you don't get things quite right.

Things my mind says	Kind things I can say to myself

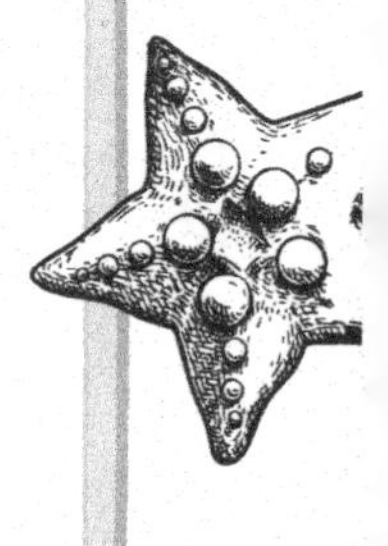

Epilogue

Dear amazing young human, well done.

Well done for having the courage to pick up this book, and well done for working your way through whatever bits you worked through.

Remember that conquering anxiety doesn't always look the way we expect it to. Sometimes it happens quickly, with bold steps. Sometimes it happens in fits and starts. Either way, working through anxiety to the life you most want to build for yourself is less about *thinking* and much, much more about *doing*. And it's not about not feeling anxious – it's actually about *not* avoiding anxiety – at the expense of a beautiful, roomy, free life when anxiety shows up.

We hope that you'll try out the practices in this book. We hope that you'll keep going, even when it's hard. We hope that you know you aren't alone. Most of all, we hope you know that you have everything you need, in your best and in your worst moments, to build a freer, more alive, and more playful and joyful life for yourself.

We believe in you.

LISA W. COYNE, PHD, is Founder and Senior Clinical Consultant of the McLean OCD Institute for Children and Adolescents, and Assistant Professor in the Department of Psychiatry at Harvard Medical School in Boston, Massachusetts, USA. She also founded and directs the New England Center for OCD and Anxiety, is fellow and past president of the Association of Contextual Behavioral Science (ACBS), and is on the Clinical and Scientific Advisory Board of the International OCD Foundation. She is co-author of *The Joy of Parenting* (with Amy Murrell), *Stuff That's Loud* (with Ben Sedley), *Acceptance and Commitment Therapy: The Clinician's Guide for Supporting Parents* (with Koa Whittingham), and *Stop Avoiding Stuff* (with Matt Boone and Jennifer Gregg).

SARAH CASSIDY, PHD, has worked as a psychologist in private practice in Ireland for more than twenty years, specializing in the assessment and treatment of emotional, behavioral, mental health, neurodevelopmental and learning differences in children and adolescents. She is Founder and Director at the Smithsfield Clinic, and Co-founder and Co-Director of the New England Centre for OCD and Anxiety, Ireland Branch. She also lectures and researches in Psychology at Maynooth University. She is a Peer Reviewed Trainer in Acceptance and Commitment Therapy, a member of the Association for Child and Adolescent Mental Health, and a Chartered Member and Council Member of the Psychological Society of Ireland. She is a Member of the Division of Clinical Child and Adolescent Psychologists of the American Psychological Association. She is the author of numerous peer-reviewed scientific articles and book chapters.